101
Exciting Activities to Do in Retirement

The Ultimate Guide to Live the Best Life After

Work: Find Out the Secrets to Make the Most

Out of Your Golden Years

By

Harold J. Wells

Table of Contents

Introduction

Welcome to "101 Exciting Activities to Do in Retirement," a guide that will take you on a journey to unlock the boundless potential of your golden years. I'm Harold J. Wells, your fellow retiree and passionate explorer of all the joys and opportunities that retirement has to offer.

As you embark on this new phase of life, you may find yourself asking, "What now?" or "How can I make the most of my retirement?" Look no further, for this book is designed to help you navigate through the exciting, sometimes daunting, but ultimately rewarding world of retirement.

My goal with this book is to inspire you, provide practical tips and advice, and ultimately help you live the fulfilling retirement you've always dreamed of. In these pages, you'll find a treasure trove of ideas and activities that cater to various interests, whether you're an outdoor enthusiast, a lifelong learner, or a creative spirit. I'll also share valuable advice on how to manage your finances and budget so you can enjoy your retirement to the fullest without worrying about breaking the bank.

One of the most important lessons I've learned in my retirement journey is that it's a time of exploration, discovery, and personal growth. It's an opportunity to redefine your identity, pursue your passions, and forge new connections with the world around you. This book will serve as your roadmap, guiding you toward a life that is rich in experiences, learning, and joy.

So, let's embark on this exciting adventure together! With an open mind and a willingness to embrace new opportunities, we'll chart a course for a retirement that is not only fun but also deeply fulfilling and meaningful. Whether you're a recent retiree or simply planning for the future, this book will equip you with the tools, inspiration, and confidence to seize the day and make the most of your golden years.

Welcome to the adventure of a lifetime!

Chapter 1: Embracing the Freedom of Retirement

It's crucial to remember that you're getting older if you want to make the most of your retirement years, since even while this is an exciting period in which you can pursue everything that interests you (and steer clear of things that don't), you are still getting older. Don't let anything stop you from moving on. If you take care of both your body and mind, age is merely a number that doesn't matter. Some of these things to do on your bucket list are reflective of new scientific findings on the prevention of Alzheimer's disease and dementia.

You may keep these disorders at bay and live a long, happy life by incorporating a number of different activities into your regular routine, despite the fact that they are frightening and difficult to predict. The majority of these adjustments to lifestyle can be made with as little effort as going out with friends, going to the gym, or tackling a crossword problem. Walking for 45 minutes three times a week has been shown to increase brain volume (specifically in the hippocampus, the part of the brain responsible for memory), and even the movement of doing simple, everyday activities like housework and cooking may make a difference in brain health in your 70s and 80s. Maintaining the ability to cook, clean, and do errands is beneficial to cognitive function in old age, so resist the urge to outsource these tasks to loved ones.

Adjusting to Life After Retirement

Adapting to change can be challenging, despite the fact that it is an unavoidable aspect of life. It could appear that life is moving at an ever-increasingly rapid pace as we become older. Your children eventually leave the house, you say goodbye to friends and loved ones, the demands on your body and health increase, and you get closer and closer to retirement. It is natural to react to these shifts with a variety of different feelings, many of which will be at odds with one another. You may, however, make the transition from working to being retired in the same way that you made the journey from youth to maturity.

Finding Purpose and Meaning in Retirement

Working is much more than just making money for many of us; it gives our lives meaning and purpose in addition to providing financial support. Your job has the potential to make you feel wanted, productive, and helpful; it may also provide goals, and it might simply provide you with a cause to leave the house on a daily basis. Having a purpose in life not only satisfies some psychological demands but also contributes to the maintenance of a healthy brain and immune system.

It is essential, once you have retired, to search for new sources of meaning in the form of activities that bring you joy and improve your life. In this regard, it can be beneficial if you are not just retiring from something but also retiring to something else; for example, you could replace your previous career with a rewarding pastime, a role as a volunteer, or ongoing study.

Instead, then immediately transitioning into retirement, many people find that making a gradual transition into full-time retirement is more beneficial. You might want to consider taking a sabbatical or an extended vacation if your employer would allow it so that you can replenish your batteries and evaluate how well you can adapt to a more sedate way of life. You can also make use of this time to evaluate how well you will be able to live off of the savings you have set up for your retirement.

You can also ease into retirement by gradually cutting back on the number of hours you put in in your current career, making a move to a part-time position, or finding some means to go into business for yourself in some manner. Part-time work is a great way to supplement your income, stay socially involved, and smooth the transition into retirement because it does not need you to put in the effort required by full-time work. In addition to giving you a sense of purpose, part-time work offers several benefits.

Navigating the Challenges of Retirement

No matter what your circumstances are, the end of your working life will bring about change; some of these adjustments will be positive, while others will be negative, unexpected, or even traumatic. For example, if your career was mentally or physically draining, left you feeling unfulfilled, or caused you to feel burned out, retiring can feel like a significant burden has been lifted off your shoulders. On the other hand, retirement may bring more difficult issues for those who took pleasure in their work, felt it to be satisfying, and centered their social lives on their careers. Things might be particularly challenging for you if you had to make concessions in your personal or family life for the sake of your job, if you were forced to retire before you felt ready, or if you have health problems that limit what you are currently able to do.

In a similar vein, your perspective on life can play a role in how effectively you manage the transition from working to being retired. If you tend to have a good outlook and are optimistic about the future, you will probably be able to adapt to the shift better than if you are prone to worry or have difficulty coping with the unpredictability of life.

The following are some common difficulties associated with retirement:

- Particularly in the first few weeks or months following retirement, having trouble "switching off" from work mentality and being able to relax.

- You are experiencing increased levels of anxiety as a result of having more time on your hands but less money to spend.

- You have a hard time finding meaningful things to do with the additional time you now have available.

- Having your identity stolen from you. Who are you now that you're not, for example, a nurse, a teacher, a designer, a salesperson, an electrician, or a driver?

- When you are away from your coworkers for an extended period of time, you may experience feelings of isolation.

- Noticing a decrease in how valuable, significant, or self-confident you feel you are becoming.

- Adapting your daily routine or finding new ways to keep your independence can be challenging now that you and your husband spend the day together at home.

- There are retirees who experience feelings of guilt since they are receiving money from a pension even if they did not actually work for it.

- Take steps to reduce your levels of stress, anxiety, and sadness.

Even if the daily grind of the commute, the deadlines, the demanding employer, and the nine-to-five routine may be done after you retire, that does not necessarily mean that your life will be devoid of stress and anxiety from that point forward. Stress at work can have a major toll on your health, especially if you are dissatisfied with your employment, but detrimental pressures can also follow you into retirement and continue to have an impact on your life.

You might be concerned about maintaining your standard of living on a fixed income, coming to terms with your worsening health, or adjusting to a new dynamic in your relationship with your partner now that you spend all day at home. Your sense of self-worth might be negatively impacted, you can feel helpless, and it could even lead to depression if you lose your identity, your routine, and your goals. Despite the difficulties you are experiencing, there are healthy methods to reduce stress and anxiety, enhance your ability to adapt to change and boost your mood, perspective, and general well-being.

Chapter 2: Pursuing Lifelong Learning

Your emotional wellbeing, physical health, and ability to establish new social connections will all improve if you continue studying throughout your life, even after you've reached retirement age. It was often claimed by Henry Ford that "anyone who stops learning is old, whether at 20 or 80." Whoever continues to educate themselves will always be young at heart. No matter how old you are, embracing a passion for learning and actively seeking out opportunities to learn new abilities is the key to keeping your brain engaged and active throughout your life.

There's no question that you should keep learning throughout your life, even after you've reached retirement age and beyond; it's beneficial to your mental health, it helps your body stay in better shape, and it facilitates the formation of new social ties. In this guide on learning how to embrace it at every stage of life, we are going to: Discuss what it means to be a learner who never stops, weigh the advantages of lifelong education, and figure out which form of education is most compatible with your retirement strategy.

As you figure out how to make the most of your retirement lifestyle, it is my sincere hope that you will pick up a thing or two along the road. Learning new things throughout your entire life is a great way to keep your mind sharp. A significant component of leading a healthy lifestyle in retirement is continuing your education throughout your life in order to keep your mind sharp.

What is Meant by "Lifelong Learning"?

Once you walk out of the school doors, you never really stop learning; thus, we may all consider ourselves to be lifelong learners. Throughout our lifetimes, we acquire new skills and information in a variety of contexts, such as learning to play an instrument or conducting research in a previously unexplored field. The only qualification necessary to graduate as a student who never stops learning is a passion for education.

Lifelong learning is a concept that does not have a set definition, but it generally refers to an innate motivation to continue learning and developing new skills, frequently outside of the context of formal schooling. In spite of this, it is still possible to participate in lifelong learning by taking classes at a higher or TAFE institution and gaining new skills. Instead, it denotes that education is pursued on one's own for the sake of one's own personal growth and fulfillment, as opposed to satisfying any kind of official requirement to finish a course of study.

This commitment to furthering one's own self-fulfillment through skill acquisition should not end after one has reached retirement age. You can give your time greater purpose and meaning by continuing your education in a subject that you are interested in and by taking advantage of opportunities to gain new skills. But the numerous advantages of learning throughout one's life don't end there!

The Benefits of Continuing to Learn in Retirement

The following are some of the benefits that can result from incorporating learning into your retirement years:

Increasing One's Self-Confidence and Personality Aspects

Participating in lifelong learning, whether in the form of enrolling in a class with other people who share your interests or carrying out your own independent research, can help you feel more assured in both your existing knowledge and your chosen fields of study. In addition, working with other people enables you to strengthen essential communication skills as well as your own emotional intelligence, both of which are skills that we carry with us throughout our entire lives.

What's crucial is that education gives your life greater purpose and meaning, and something as basic as learning how to use an iPad may be considered learning.

Enhancing Your Mental Powers & Health

If you don't use your brain, you run the danger of having memory problems, which can be exacerbated by mental inactivity. Think of your brain as a muscle; if you don't utilize it, it will atrophy over time if you don't keep it active. It is possible to increase your overall mental wellbeing, memory retention, and problem-solving skills by exercising your brain through the process of learning. This can include expanding your knowledge about a subject that you are particularly interested in or training yourself in a new skill.

Acquiring New Social Contacts

Participating in a class that encourages lifelong learning puts you in an excellent position to forge new relationships with people from all walks of life. Even if you are not a very outgoing person, there is a good chance that the other people in the room share some of your interests. This makes it much simpler to connect with these people and develop new friendships. It is crucial for people in Australia who are approaching retirement to meet new people who share their interests, as this provides an alternate social outlet to the time spent with coworkers in the workplace.

Creating New Passions and Interests for Oneself

Trying a new pastime for the first time after retiring might be a frightening prospect; after all, if you've never engaged in the activity before, how do you know if you'll enjoy it now? The gift of additional time is only one of the perks that come with leaving a career behind. If you have always wanted to learn a new language or become an expert with a nine iron, think of each new day as an opportunity to learn something new and expand your skill set!

When you combine learning with some well-deserved rest and relaxation, you stand to reap a lot of benefits, and they are only the beginning! Continuing your education when you retire is the ideal chance to devote yourself to mastering a talent you've always been interested in but never had the time to develop fully.

Exploring Education & Learning Opportunities

Building on your desire to acquire new skills or knowledge throughout your life is the foundation of lifelong learning, which can take place in either a formal or an informal context. Depending on how social you are and how much money you have saved up for retirement, you can continue your education in one of these three methods as an older adult:

Degrees Awarded by Universities

There are a lot of elderly people in Australia who never got the chance to pursue higher education when they were younger, so retirement is the perfect time for them to make that goal come true. The fact that a man in his nineties was able to receive a master's degree from the University of Melbourne demonstrates that it is never too late to acquire new knowledge, as evidenced by a recent report from ABC. Finding a tertiary education institution and a program that caters to your lifestyle and interests can be made easier with the assistance of resources such as the Good Universities Guide.

Communal Educational Institutions

Community classes could be the answer for individuals who desire the variety of course options and the social involvement of a formal course but do not want to pay the fees associated with attending university. Institutions can be found all around the Sydney metropolitan area and in the Illawarra region that offers a formal training program or academic curriculum that caters to any and all interests. Some examples of this institution are Sydney Community College. Maintaining an active interest in furthering your education will put you in the greatest position to make the most of your retirement years.

Expand Your Horizons: Reading and Mind-Challenging Activities

Formal education is only one component of the larger goal of lifelong learning, which also includes the pursuit of activities that keep one's mind active outside of the classroom. Reading, whether it be in the form of books, periodicals, or newspapers, keeps your mind more active than doing sedentary hobbies like watching television. Even if you only read for an hour a day instead of watching television for an hour, you will see improvements in your brain capacity. In addition, engaging in mental challenges like Sudoku or participating in a training course will assist you in getting the most out of your formally structured learning opportunities.

Minimize your Stress

Because of too much stress, all of us have had the experience of being unable to think properly in either our professional or personal life. Reducing the amount of stress you experience throughout your retirement years will benefit you in more ways than one. Additionally, it will boost your ability to find solutions to issues and concentrate on the job at hand. When attempting to learn something new, you will find that both of these skills are absolutely necessary.

Chapter 3: Traveling and Exploring New Places

Although not everyone's retirement savings will allow them to spend their summers in Australia and their winters on the slopes of Aspen, there are plenty of other areas in the United States that are just as deserving of exploration. How often do you tell yourself that you'll visit local attractions in your city or day trip destinations eventually, one day when you have time, but you never actually do? It is not unusual for visitors to a destination to see more, participate in more activities, and know more about the location than the residents do. Why should one, therefore, wait any longer?

Planning your Dream Vacation or Adventure

Planning for retirement should include giving some thought to the activities you would like to pursue once you are no longer working. In addition, if you are able to be as comprehensive and clear as possible regarding how, when, where, why, and with whom you wish to travel, you will increase the likelihood that you will be successful.

- Do you have a list of places you want to visit before you die?
- Do you plan to take one trip a month, approximately? Once a calendar year?

- Are you pondering impromptu excursions in order to take advantage of opportunities to save money? Or are there particular locations that you wish to visit?

- Who will go with you? Spouse? Friends? Grandkids? Siblings?

- What compels you to embark on this journey?

-

Come to an Understanding With Your Partner

The lack of communication between spouses is a frequently neglected part of retirement preparation. According to the findings of a survey conducted by Fidelity Investments, many married couples have a very difficult time addressing topics related to retirement planning and other aspects of financial planning.

In addition, it is not uncommon for spouses to have completely different concepts of what they want to get out of retirement and how they want to pay for everything. Is retirement travel important to you? What kinds of activities does your spouse have in mind for their golden years? Get some advice on how to broach the subject of retiring with your partner.

Consider More Exotic Locales

It's possible that you have a few favorite places that you want to visit again, but it's also a good idea to include some incredibly unique places on your travel wish list for when you retire. Let's face it: as we become older, we've already had a lot of life experiences and seen a lot of things. It's possible that some days you'll feel as though nothing can surprise you anymore. Traveling, on the other hand, is one way to see something brand new and exciting. When viewed from this angle, traveling can practically provide the opportunity to experience life through the eyes of a child, which is to say, to wonder and be amazed at things that are brand new. The best part is that it has been demonstrated through research that engaging in new experiences of this kind helps to keep our minds more active.

"The greatest reward and luxury of travel, in my opinion, is to be able to experience everyday things as if for the first time, to be in a position in which almost nothing is so familiar that it is taken for granted," said one traveler. "It is to be able to experience everyday things as if for the first time."

Search for Elder Discounts at Local Hotels and Airlines

You are probably aware that the majority of hotel chains provide elderly citizens with discounts of 10-20 percent on their room rates. These discounts are comparable to those provided by AAA and are typically easy to locate on the websites of local hotels. It's possible that you are unaware that several airlines provide senior discounts as well. On the other hand, it is not as widespread as it once was, and the senior discount might not be the best value that can be found. These are some of the airlines that are currently providing discounts:

- AARP members can receive a discount on their flights with British Airways.
- There are various flights on which Delta Airlines provides discounts. To find out which flights are available and to make

reservations at these rates, you will need to contact them by phone at 1-800-221-1212.

- Southwest also provides discounts for older citizens; however, these fares can only be purchased by calling the following number: 1-800-I-FLY-SWA (1-800-435-9792).

- Similar to Delta, United Airlines provides discounts for passengers over the age of 65 on select flights. Dial 1-800-241-6522 and ask for customer service.

Get on the Open Road

RV sales have been soaring recently, with the majority of customers falling in the age range of 50–69. Twenty-four percent of retirees believe that taking a trip in an RV is highly tempting to them at this stage of their life. And hipster vagabonds frequently travel in campervans as their mode of transportation of choice. On the other hand, senior citizens might be the most appealing demographic for these mobile homes. These vehicles can serve as both your mode of transportation and you're lodging all in one convenient package. Some individuals even go so far as to sell their houses and move their households onto the road.

Excellent Resources to Consider for Road Trip

One of life's greatest pleasures is going on a road trip, and it doesn't matter if you want to take a cross-country vacation that lasts a few weeks or if you just want to go to the next town over for the day.

The following is a list of excellent resources that can be used to locate fascinating detours along the way:

- Listings of 1,600 swimming holes around the United States and Canada can be found on the Swimming Holes website.

- Roadside Attractions: Enter your route and find some strange places to stop along the way.

- Maps with fantastic treks, camping, excursions, and more are available through The Outdoor Project.

- Roadfood.com: The Stern brothers, Jan and Michael, are often considered to be the most well-known advocates for eating in roadside restaurants. Their website, RoadFood.com, will assist you in finding local restaurants, cafés, diners, and other eating establishments that specialize in regional cuisine and are casual and economical.

- GasBuddy is an application that allows users to locate the petrol station in their immediate area that offers the lowest price.

- Roadtrippers is an app that helps travelers identify interesting places to stop along their journey.

- "There is nothing behind me, and everything in front of me, as it always is on the road," the driver said.

Go Last Minute and Save

When you have a job, travel plans often have to be crammed into the few days off that you have. When it comes to travel after retirement, you have a great deal more flexibility to take advantage of possibilities and offers that come up at the last minute. There are a good number of websites and mobile applications that can be of use to you when planning excursions on the spur of the moment, including the following:

- The application known as Hotel Tonight is called Hotel Tonight. They purchase unsold inventory from hotels for the night in question and then make it available to users of the app at a steep discount.

- Intrepid Travel is a tour operator that can plan trips for you. You can look at their offers at the very last minute.

- Groupon: Groupon offers a wide variety of coupons good for discounts on a wide variety of activities and experiences. They also have some deals till the very last minute.

- Lastminute.com is primarily concerned with offering last-minute offers for destinations throughout Europe.

- Travelzoo's mission is to provide its customers with the best prices available from the top companies.

- Be careful; using Google Flights has the potential to become mildly addicted. If you use Google Flights and leave the destination field blank while entering your departure location and dates, the search engine will return a list of the lowest possible airfares that are accessible to you.

Set Aside Some Time For Planning

Even though spur-of-the-moment excursions might be thrilling and entertaining, you run the risk of missing out on what researchers consider to be the most rewarding aspect of vacationing. You might believe that the most enjoyable aspect is anything like taking in the scene at a historic landmark, letting your toes sink into the beach, or inhaling the aroma of freshly baked bread from a nearby bakery. Nevertheless, the results of this study indicate that the most enjoyable portion of your journey occurs long before you even board the airplane.

The study found that being excited about a vacation by preparing for it and thinking about it made people happier than actually going on the trip. In the spirit of planning, you should make sure that your retirement plans include a budget for the trips you intend to take when you retire. The New Retirement Planner provides you with the ability to include funds for travel as a component of both your monthly and annual budgets. Alternately, you can detail one-time costs associated with particular vacations.

Give Volunteer Travel A Shot

Voluntourism, often known as volunteering while traveling, is becoming an increasingly popular kind of travel for seniors in their retirement years. Consider volunteering with one of these well-known organizations if you want to see the world and yet feel like you're making a difference at the same time:

- Habitat for Humanity, an initiative of the Earthwatch Institute
- Global Vision International Volunteer
- The International Peace Corps

Bring Along The Grandchildren

If going on vacation is the activity that individuals look forward to the most once they retire, then spending time with their grandchildren is likely to come in second. So why not bring them both together? Taking your grandchildren on an adventure together while also creating unforgettable memories is one of the best ways to spend quality time with them. Make sure that they are involved in the planning of the trip so that it will be a success (you may also want to ask their parents for their thoughts).

Tips for Affordable and Sustainable Travel

We can all agree that seeing the world is one of the most eye-opening and empowering things you can do. To travel is to encounter different people, customs, and traditions. Travel broadens one's horizons and broadens one's thoughts. However, eco-friendly travel options are increasingly in demand. As budget-minded globetrotters, we need to adopt more environmentally friendly practices and reduce our environmental impact. One of the things pressing us now is climate change, which brings with it hotter weather, more frequent and intense wildfires, higher sea levels, and thawing glaciers. Research indicates that tourism accounts for 8% of global greenhouse gas emissions. A person's carbon footprint increases by two to three tons while traveling back and forth between Europe and the United States. That's a major deal!

Therefore, it is evident that we must develop greener travel habits. But how do you achieve this while still keeping your travel expenses low? Check out the advice below to learn how to travel in a more environmentally responsible manner.

- Lighten your load: Pack less to reduce luggage weight, choose eco-friendly transport options, and enjoy more freedom during your travels.

- Limit airplane use: Opt for budget airlines when necessary, and consider alternative travel methods like buses or trains when time allows.

- Walk or bike: Choose greener transportation methods for short distances, benefit from improved health, and lower your environmental impact.

- Longer stays: Spend more time in each location to reduce your carbon footprint, save money, and immerse yourself in local culture.

- Eco-friendly hostels: Stay in environmentally responsible accommodations, cut costs, and connect with other travelers and locals.

- House-sitting: Save money on lodging, experience local life, and help others by taking care of their homes and pets while they're away.

- Reusable water bottle: Bring your own water bottle to reduce plastic waste and encourage more sustainable packaging practices.

- Neighborhood eateries: Support local businesses, enjoy authentic cuisine, and minimize carbon emissions from imported ingredients.
- Avoid disposables: Invest in reusable utensils and plates to save money, reduce your carbon footprint, and decrease plastic waste.

Making the Most of your Travel Experiences

You've finally reached retirement age or are very close to it, and you're probably itching to start planning that long-awaited trip. It's always helpful to have some travel information and some ways to save money on hand, whether you intend to visit every national park in the United States, go to different countries, or stick mostly to beach vacations.

Review these seven suggestions for traveling in retirement before packing your most supple walking shoes.

Take Advantage of Off-Peak Travel Seasons After Retirement

By traveling outside of the high season, you can save a lot of money on lodgings of all types. For instance, in the United States, you can save hundreds of dollars on lodging and transportation costs by taking a trip a few weeks before or after Memorial Day or Labour Day.

Use the Low Monthly Rental Rates for Vacations

Do you wish to spend your vacation leisurely getting to know the area? Think about reserving a month at a vacation rental service like Airbnb,

Vrbo, or somewhere else. You'll have plenty of time to settle in, get to know the neighborhood and other visitors, and see all the sights. You can save money on food by cooking at the vacation rental instead of eating out every meal. In addition, a lot of holiday rentals have special monthly rates.

Three Ways to Save Money as You Age

It's possible that your eternal youth makes you forget to ask for elder discounts. Hotels, restaurants, tour operators, stores, car rental agencies, and airlines all offer discounts to seniors, which can add up to significant savings that can be put towards activities, meals out, and extended trips.

Pick Tourist Attractions That Old People Love to Visit

No matter how much you adore Florida, you probably won't enjoy your spring break there because of all the college students. If you want to take a trip where you can hang out with other retirees and older adults, check up locations and towns with a sizable senior population or tourist hotspots that cater to this demographic. Businesses, restaurants, and shops that appeal to a more senior clientele are common in tourist areas that are popular with retirees.

Base Your Vacations on Things You Enjoy Doing at Home

Vacation spots with world-class golf courses are ideal for the avid golfer. Do you have a passion for the past? If so, plan a trip to a city where you may take a guided bus or foot excursions, as well as see interesting historical places. Plan a trip to a destination hosting a convention or conference related to your interests and hobbies.

Rent Out Your Home When on Vacations

Do you intend to spend your retirement years in a warm-weather vacation rental? If you're looking to save money on a two- or three-month rental, consider listing your house on Airbnb or another vacation rental website. Airbnb provides hosts with liability insurance of up to $1 million and damage protection of up to the same amount, so you can feel safe renting out your home. Because they depend on hosts' reviews to be selected for future rentals, Airbnb guests have the incentive to leave your house in good condition.

Join a Touring Group

Group travel is a great way for retirees to meet new people while taking advantage of travel perks like guided tours, group discounts at attractions, and shared meals and activities. Look for a guided tour that suits your interests. A group trip can be a good option if you want to save money and feel more secure than you would if you traveled alone or with a partner to learn about the art, history, and culture of a foreign country.

Chapter 4: Hobbies and Activities

Find interests that complement your way of living. According to Ari Parker, a leading licensed Medicare advisor at Chapter in Phoenix, "hobbies are wonderful because they offer people a way to contribute to their communities, find new friends, learn new skills, or just have a great time enjoying a much-loved experience" in retirement. As one author puts it, "Hobbies can be a fulfilling way for many people across the country to spend time doing things they enjoy with people they love."

Many people in the United States who are on the cusp of retirement have sought Parker's advice. What matters most, according to Parker, is that you select a hobby that fits your unique character. While taking up a new language can be the ideal pastime for some, others might like enrolling in a pottery class. Some people like social gatherings where they may learn something new, like salsa dancing, while others might rather do something more intellectual, like join a book club.

Benefits of Hobbies and Activities in Retirement

After a lifetime of toil, you now enjoy the fruits of your labor: retirement. The time has come to cash in your chips. Now you don't have to put as much effort into productivity-oriented things. Spend your time and energy on things that make you happy instead. Keep reading to find out why you need pastimes in retirement.

Maintains a Youthful Attitude

Whether it's restoring classic cars or crocheting, having a hobby you enjoy can make the transition to retirement much easier. It might even keep your spirit young! Regaining your pep and (hopefully) a sense of purpose can be facilitated by engaging in an activity that is designed simply for your enjoyment.

Use What You Know and What You Can Do

As you gain experience and wisdom, you come to understand that fulfillment is within your grasp at any time. All you have to do is seize any opportunity that comes your way. It might be challenging to attempt new activities as a young adult because of responsibilities like starting a family, going to school at night, and working overtime to grow in your career. You have the luxury of time, money, and freedom to explore new avenues until you discover an activity that truly inspires you.

Learn a Fresh Concept

Hobbies are great for maintaining both your physical and mental well-being, and they also provide excellent opportunities for growth and development. We as humans are always on the lookout for something to push us to our limits, and trying something new could be just the thing to do. When you're feeling bored or stuck in a rut, it can be helpful to take a step outside of your comfort zone and do something you truly enjoy. Give some thought to past interests. Perhaps some kayaking, horseback riding, or gardening? The activity need not be strenuous in terms of physical exertion. Playing games that challenge one's mind, like checkers or sudoku, can also help increase endorphin release.

Let Go and Chill Out

Hobbies are a great way to de-stress in a positive and productive way when life gets stressful. Enjoyable activities have been shown to reduce blood pressure. Are you a fan of sugary treats? Master the art of baking delicious sweets. How do you feel about tranquility? You may go bird watching, fishing, or gardening. The goal is to associate a pleasurable task with something you enjoy doing in order to take your mind off of whatever is stressing you out.

A Healthy Lifestyle is Promoted Through Hobbies

Hobbies are fun at any age, but engaging in them as an adult has several positive effects on health. Regularly engaging in a hobby, be it gardening or playing the piano, can boost your immune system. Increasing physical activity is good for everyone, but if you're always sick or have mobility issues, a pastime may be just what you need to start feeling well again.

Low-cost Hobby Ideas and Activities

One of the first and biggest issues retirees confront is figuring out how to make the most of their extra time. There is more time to devote to family and perhaps a few hours of part-time employment each week, but a lot of that spare time can be put to good use with a satisfying pastime.

1. Pickleball: A sport that resembles tennis but is played on a smaller court. It is well-suited to retirees because it is typically played in big, mixed-partner "open play" sessions. Many senior communities have pickleball courts available at no cost with advance scheduling. Professional pickleball lessons are available for about $50 per hour.

2. Writing: Journaling is a helpful emotional release, and writing your memoirs can help your grandchildren and great-grandchildren understand who you are and what your life is about. Sharing lessons you have learned can also help others.

3. Dealing with Stocks: Learning how to trade stocks can help retirees increase the amount of money they have available to support their lifestyle expenses. Investing in stocks is a great strategy to boost retirement savings. Learning a new skill and managing one's funds are two of the key benefits of this activity.

4. Gardening: Growing your own veggies and herbs is a great way for retirees to ensure they continue to eat a healthy, balanced diet full of fresh, colorful produce. Gardening can be as simple as planting a few vegetables in your backyard or as extensive as building a greenhouse for more plant cultivation.

5. Walking: Exercise can help keep retirees young both physically and mentally and help extend quality years while cutting down on hospital visits. Walking is an excellent option as it can be started by anyone, including those who were not physically fit during their working years. It's a great way to meet new people and get involved in the community.

6. Golf: Golf provides retirees with a feeling of purpose and fulfillment by facilitating social interaction, intellectual stimulation, and physical activity. It addresses all four categories of retirement life, making it an ideal hobby for those in their golden years.

7. Volunteering: Volunteering is a great way to help non-profits with limited resources and enrich the lives of volunteers themselves. It can also force retirees out of their shells and into the world, helping them engage in something they enjoy.

8. Mentoring: Retirees possess experiences that most individuals in our society don't have, and they can provide a fresh angle from which to impart information that might be difficult to learn in a conventional classroom. Mentoring business executives, young adults, and students can be a fulfilling and charitable activity for retirees.

Suggestions for Exploring New Hobbies and Activities

In place of rocking chairs, we now see seniors riding bicycles and driving golf carts. Today's retirees aren't satisfied with a quiet life; they want excitement, purpose, and opportunities for growth out of their golden years. The typical lifespan of a retiree is 18. You can get a lot done in that amount of time. You'll be retiring for quite some time, so you might as well start enjoying life in other ways.

Hobbies are more than just something you do to pass the time. The appropriate activities could extend your life and improve your health. Here are ten fantastic suggestions for filling your retirement years.

Restart Your Education

It's never too late to start or finish a degree in your senior year of high school, regardless of whether you've already had a fantastic college experience or your higher education objectives were sidelined by the responsibilities of daily life. The thought of returning to school while also working and caring for a family can be overwhelming.

Because of your retirement, you'll be able to relax more. That means you can focus entirely on your schoolwork without worrying about anything else and potentially excel academically. Senior citizen discounts are available at several two-year institutions and four-year universities. Some schools offer free auditing for seniors.

Travel

There will never be a better opportunity to travel than right now. You are free to take a trip without worrying about your boss disapproving or your children complaining in the car. Here are a few terrific low-cost vacation choices:

- Getting a mobile home, either to buy or to rent, and driving around the country.
- Camping trips to state and federal preserves, a lifetime pass to America's national parks costs just $80 for seniors.

- Swapping locations, you could try exchanging residences with people in different towns or even different countries.

- Apartment sharing, Airbnb, and VRBO are two websites that provide alternatives to expensive hotels and resorts for lower prices.

Exit the House

It's now warm enough to take advantage of all the outdoor activities you've been meaning to do. You need not be a pioneer to appreciate the time spent in nature. Among the best choices are:

- Create or enlarge your existing garden: Gardening is a wonderful way to spend time with others. Participate in seed swaps, gardening meetups, or a garden club.

- Hone your abilities in nature: Learn to fish for the first time, enroll in a class on medicinal herbs, or brush up on your outdoor survival skills.

- Do something active outside: The pace of golf is suitable for most elderly people. You can get your feet wet on a beginner's green and then work your way up to the more difficult ones as your skills and stamina improve.

- Get a pet and spend more time outside: A stray dog you took in from the pound might like going fishing and hiking with you.

- Consider organizing a camping trip, a weekly picnic, or a monthly scavenger hunt as outdoor activities to enjoy with friends and family.

- Participate in geocaching: It's a fantastic opportunity to socialize in natural surroundings. You can tackle this on your own or with a group of other geocachers.

There is no need for a gym membership or tedious at-home aerobics programs when you can simply go outside and start moving about. Even in your older years, exercise is essential. Dementia and heart disease risks are lowered, diabetes is slowed in its progression, and mental health problems like depression are avoided. Get up and move by doing something you enjoy.

Develop Your Talents

It requires time and works to acquire new abilities. Perhaps this explains why you've never learned how to play the guitar or speak Spanish. Now that you have more free time, you may put that money toward bettering yourself. For suggestions, browse the course listings at your local community college or consider paying for private instruction. The benefits of acquiring new knowledge and abilities can last a lifetime. Keeping your mind sharp and engaged is good for your health and might even reduce your chance of developing dementia.

Confront Fresh Faces

It's never too late to expand your social circle. Relationships are the foundation of a fulfilling life, whether you're seven or seventy. Spend time and effort cultivating new relationships, whether platonic or romantic. Among the best approaches to expanding social circles are:

- Participating in regional interests communities online: Here, you may get to know the locals online before ever meeting them.

- Taking part in activities at a nearby senior center.

- Seminars about subjects that fascinate you.

- To sign up for Meetup.

- Having conversations with intriguing strangers. You can gain a lot by taking a small risk. Meet the bookseller or barista who, in their golden years, appears a touch bored.

- Participate in a senior adventure organization that offers trips, wine tastings, and other activities.

- Get on a cruise as a senior citizen.

Spend your Time More Lavishly

It's one of retirement's best-kept secrets that you can enjoy a high standard of living on a relatively modest income. With beautiful houses, manicured grounds, and amenities like swimming pools and tennis courts, senior living communities provide a turnkey solution to the challenges of retirement. The responsibilities, costs, and uncertainty of home ownership are removed when you move into a senior living community. The proceeds from a property sale can also be put toward other goals or used as a legacy. Then maybe it's time to stop pinching pennies and start spending like it's the high life.

Chapter 5: Volunteering and Community Involvement

Don't dive headfirst into the nonprofit sector without first laying the groundwork, especially if you expect to be financially compensated for your efforts. When people reach retirement age, they tend to become less active than they were before retirement. A cohort research indicated that retirees who were less active before retirement were more likely to remain inactive afterward. The motivation to leave the house and maintain an active lifestyle has diminished. The deleterious effects of a sedentary lifestyle on physical health are well-documented. The danger of health problems increases with age; thus, seniors should engage in regular exercise. It might be anything from signing up for a Zumba class to going for long walks.

People's natural reluctance to engage in physical activity can be overcome by the moral support provided by group workouts. Seniors are more likely to maintain their exercise routine if they do so in a group setting. Seeing other seniors going through the same exercise routine would motivate them to join in. New friendships formed during group workouts can help strengthen ties within the community. Making new friends is important for everyone, but it can be especially helpful for seniors who have just experienced a loss. Grief and isolation can be lessened via contact with the outside world and other people.

Volunteering and Philanthropy Opportunities

The word "retirement" is used to conjure up mental pictures of doting grandparents cradling their grandchildren on their front porches. However, with both sexes living longer and in better health into their older years, retirement has become a very busy period of life, with many retirees devoting themselves to causes and interests that they had to put on the back burner while focusing on their careers or raising families. In 2011, the first of the "boomer" generation will reach 65, and their enthusiasm, life experience, and professional knowledge will be invaluable to nonprofits of all stripes [source: Grinberg]. There are many options for retirees who want to give back to their communities by volunteering their time and energy to worthy causes.

Based on research into volunteer opportunities, the accessibility of those opportunities, and the openness of associated organizations to retired volunteers, I've compiled a list of the top 10 volunteer pursuits for seniors. Is participating in any of these volunteer opportunities something you could like during retirement? Find out by reading on!

Humanity's Habitat

With the help of those in need, Habitat for Humanity constructs and renovates basic, low-cost houses. Building houses and a sense of pride and community for the new homeowners and the neighborhood go hand in hand when Habitat volunteers work side by side with people who have qualified to buy a Habitat for Humanity home. Habitat for Humanity International is a Christian organization that serves people of all religions and backgrounds in the Americas, Africa, the Middle East, Europe, and Asia. On construction sites, in disaster-stricken areas, and in Habitat for Humanity's affiliate offices, you can find a lot of elderly and semi-retired people giving their time and energy. The majority of the 6,000 registered "RV Care-A-Vanners," volunteers who drive their own RVs to Habitat for Humanity's homebuilding projects around the United States, are retirees. RV Care-A-Vanners are self-funded. However, their mileage and other service-related travel costs may be deductible.

Supporting Active Duty Personnel, Veterans, and Their Families

Military retirees and civilian retirees who want to help out and express their appreciation for the military have many options. Greeting troops returning from overseas tours, making hot coffee in USO offices, and providing warm meals and warm blankets to troops on airport layovers while they wait for flights home are just a few examples of how USO volunteers help fulfill the organization's mission to improve the quality of life for military personnel and their families in the United States and around the world.

The Military Order of the Purple Heart's Veterans Affairs Volunteer Service (VAVS) Program helps veterans and others get VA health care. VAVS volunteers also work with the National Cemetery Administration to create and preserve memorials for fallen military members.

Educating Young Minds

The benefits of volunteering with children may be felt more keenly by retirees who are separated from their grandchildren because of distance or because they are waiting for their adult offspring to have children of their own. Volunteers 55 and older can participate in the Senior Corps Foster Grandparent program to work with kids at Head Start programs, schools, and other youth facilities [source: Senior Corps]. Big Brothers Big Sisters is an organization that pairs adult volunteers ("bigs") with children who could benefit from having a positive role model in their lives.

Volunteers are an integral part of the staff in many children's hospitals, where they help with tasks such as tutoring patients, reading aloud to them, supervising play areas, and providing support to families in any way they can. A background check and a commitment to volunteering for a set number of hours per week for a set period of time (often three, six, or twelve months) are standard requirements for most positions working with children.

Volunteering with kids can be not only rewarding but also lucrative in specific situations: A rising number of public school systems offer seniors a rebate on property taxes in exchange for their time helping in the classroom, and some foster grandparent volunteers are eligible to receive a tax-free hourly stipend.

Vacations for Volunteers

Retirees with the leisure and means to travel are increasingly looking for experiences that will allow them to give back to society while also broadening their horizons. Volunteer holidays, sometimes known as "voluntourism" or "service learning," can be arranged to suit participants of varying experience levels and areas of expertise. Previously known as Elderhostel, Road Scholar now organizes "service learning" trips that can last anywhere from five days to three weeks. Volunteers can assist students at schools on the Navajo Reservation, work to restore historical places, safeguard coral reefs and endangered wildlife, and even go on archaeological digs in search of long-extinct species through these programs.

About a third of the volunteers with Global Volunteers, which offers "Adventures in Service" assignments ranging from one week to twenty-four weeks in communities across the United States and internationally, are "Boomers." At the invitation and supervision of local leaders, volunteers in this organization may find themselves teaching English, giving medical care, building or repairing homes, or working with children and teenagers in need.

Aid for the Hungry

Even in times of economic prosperity, families in the United States and around the world deal with hunger and malnutrition. The need for hunger alleviation is especially great during times of recession and high unemployment. There has been a steady increase in the number of families in need of food aid and an equally steady increase in the number of elderly citizens willing to help. Nearly 20% of the clients serviced by Northwest Harvest, a hunger relief charity serving all of Washington state, are over the age of 55, and the majority of volunteers are over the age of 65. Meals on Wheels has been a mainstay of senior service for decades, with volunteers aged 60 and up delivering nutritious meals to homebound elders in all 50 states and the District of Columbia. More than a million meals are delivered daily by as many as 1.7 million volunteers, many of them are retirees. Retirees help end hunger by working as volunteers at food banks or by growing food for donation to those in need through community gardens.

Aid in Time of Need

Natural disasters of various kinds have been thrust into the spotlight in recent years by occurrences like the 2010 Haiti earthquake, the 2011 Japan earthquake and tsunami, and the 2011 Alabama and Georgia tornadoes. When natural disasters strike in the United States or elsewhere across the world, Red Cross volunteers are among the first to respond. Volunteers are needed for many aspects of disaster relief, including but not limited to handling supplies, contributions, administrative chores, and offering comfort and aid to survivors.

Guide or Docent

In retirement, many people are able to devote themselves full-time to volunteer work or to further their own education in areas that have always interested them. Docent programs are common at museums, universities, and other public and private institutions, and they teach volunteers how to give tours, maintain landmarks, and educate the public. Volunteers can gain valuable experience in a wide variety of fields by working at institutions, including botanical gardens, museums, and conservation groups.

Volunteer opportunities exist in many fields, and even those that may appear obscure to a retiree are often pleasantly surprising. In Kentucky, the largest equestrian-themed park needs volunteers to do everything from driving and maintaining ancient steam cars to rehabilitating birds of prey to giving tours.

Politics and Elections

Generation X has a long history of action, from the Civil Rights Movement and the fight for the Equal Rights Amendment to rallies against the Vietnam War, the Gulf War, and nuclear weapons. Volunteering for a political campaign, grassroots movement, or political action committee for a candidate or cause that they believe will feel like coming home for many retirees.

Regardless of your political leanings, you can always find a campaign that could use your help making phone calls, knocking on doors, circulating petitions, or organizing demonstrations. National websites like idealist.org and Volunteer Match can help you identify other causes and individuals that resonate with your ideas, and even local politicians usually have websites outlining the volunteer opportunities within their campaigns.

Advocate in the Law

All sorts of organizations require legal counsel, whether to represent their constituents in court or to represent the organizations themselves in contract negotiations, lawsuits, or other civil or commercial problems. Volunteer attorneys may be asked to represent foster kids, members of underrepresented groups, or victims of domestic violence. Volunteer lawyers also help promote human rights and economic growth on behalf of environmental organizations, public land trusts, animal rights groups, and governments in poor countries. Senior citizens who have practiced law make excellent additions to the boards of directors and administrative staff of charitable organizations.

Charities Dedicated To Helping

Volunteers are desperately needed by local animal shelters, rescues, and humane organizations in a variety of capacities, including animal care, fundraising, administration, and pet rescue in the aftermath of disasters like floods, fires, and hurricanes. It's possible that retirees who have the resources to care for an animal could take in a stray pet as a "foster parent" until the pet's permanent home is located. And for animal enthusiasts who don't want the responsibility of a pet of their own, working with animals can provide that cuddly fix. Pet owners may also want to think about enrolling their animals in a pet therapy training

42

program so that they can visit people in facilities such as hospitals, nursing homes, and hospices. Animal shelters, like other non-profits, require the services of lawyers, grant writers, and even graphic designers in order to spread the word about the importance of animal protection.

Community Impact and Beyond

Following are some ways that can help you make a difference in the community and beyond:

Helping others Learn

Assuming you are a retired educator, you can fill this void with your extensive knowledge and expertise. Tutors are needed for kids' programs at your public library or school district's foundation. The GED exam is not the only rite of passage for which many adults require assistance.

Transportation for the Elderly

Volunteers with open schedules are in high demand by community organizations that work with the elderly so that they can transport clients to necessary appointments and errands. You might make a new acquaintance while assisting someone in need of medical attention.

In Defense of Library Services

Volunteers are essential to libraries since they help patrons arrange books, staff events, and educate children and adults about the library's resources. If you're interested in volunteering, but can only spare a few hours a month, to begin with, contact your local branch to learn about available opportunities.

Giving One's Time to a Food Bank

Nonprofits and churches typically rely on volunteer labor to run their operations. Fundraising, food collection, data entry, and client service are all areas where they could use some help.

Rescue Animal Care

Volunteering at a local animal shelter is a great way to show your undying affection for homeless cats and dogs. Volunteers are also needed to assist with administrative duties, fund-raising, and other operational duties.

How to Get Appointed as a Court-Appointed Advocate

To prevent children who have been abused or neglected from falling through the cracks of an already overburdened legal and social service system or from spending too much time in an unsuitable group or foster homes, judges choose community members to serve as court-appointed special advocates (CASAs).

Chapter 6: Wellness and Self-Care

It's possible that by the time you reach the age when you can retire, you'll be comfortable with the thought of spending your days relaxing and engaging in activities that bring you joy. Even while those things are obviously significant, you also need to pay attention to your health over the long run. Because of the changes that occur in our immune systems as we get older, they no longer function as effectively as they once did. Because of this, it is imperative that we make an effort to be physically active, involved with people, and emotionally and spiritually balanced.

The Importance of Prioritizing Wellness in Retirement

Many people look forward to retirement so they can finally unwind and stop worrying about making ends meet. However, it's also a time of profound upheaval and transition, which can bring its own set of mental and bodily stresses. This is why taking care of yourself during retirement is so important for having a happy and healthy golden year. The term "wellness" refers to a state of complete mental, emotional, social, and physiological health. You may improve your quality of life, open yourself up to new experiences, and give your life direction by concentrating on these things.

Physical Health

Maintaining a healthy body is important at any age. In retirement, when the effects of aging on movement and health are more noticeable, this becomes an issue of paramount importance. Keeping up a healthy lifestyle with regular exercise, a well-balanced diet, and sufficient sleep is essential for a long, productive life.

If you want to become in better shape, try doing things like walking, swimming, cycling, and yoga. These routines can improve quality of life by assisting with weight control, cardiovascular health, and bone density maintenance.

Emotional Health

Many retirees struggle emotionally because they feel they've lost their sense of self and their reason for living once they stop working. Taking care of one's mental and emotional wellbeing requires making new social connections, such as through volunteering or joining a group. In addition, many people improve their mental health by consulting a trained specialist. Isolation, loneliness, anxiety, and depression are all sensations that can be helped by therapy, counseling, or support groups.

Social Health

Because of the importance of social connections to one's sense of fulfillment, retirement can be a time of great opportunity to make new friends and strengthen old ones. Join a reading club, go to some cultural events, or become involved with the community to broaden your social circle. Having a strong social network to lean on as you face the ups and downs of life is crucial to thriving and living a happy, fulfilling life. Keeping in touch with loved ones through means such as phone conversations, video chats, and in-person visits can help one feel more at home in their own skin.

Intellectual Health

In retirement, when mental inactivity can hasten cognitive deterioration, it is especially crucial to maintain intellectual health by keeping the mind busy and engaged. You may try doing things like reading, acquiring a new skill or language, or taking classes to advance your education. Engaging in intellectual activities is one way to maintain social ties and discover new passions. Having a feeling of meaning in one's life is essential to one's health and happiness.

Staying Active, Healthy, and Happy in Retirement Ideas

Here are some suggestions you can utilize to keep yourself busy and healthy in retirement.

Get Some Sleep

Though it goes against common sense to recommend getting more shut-eye as a means to improve your fitness, the truth is that adequate rest is vital to your mental clarity, emotional stability, and physical well-being. Older adults need between 7 and 9 hours of sleep per night, according to the National Institute on Aging, in order to function at their best.

Acquire Some New Abilities

It has been proven that learning new abilities, even something as simple as learning how to use Facebook, can have a profound effect on cognitive performance and, in particular, memory retention. Learning a new skill or taking up a new hobby in retirement might help you stay mentally and physically active (depending on the hobby or activity).

Maintaining and Building Friendships in Retirement

Maintaining your social networks after retirement may be crucial to your health. It's natural for those bonds to weaken now that you're out of employment, but there's still much you can do to keep in touch with old friends and make new ones. Depression and social isolation are particularly common among the elderly. Planning social events, maintaining regular religious or spiritual practices, or participating in group intellectual pursuits are all great ways to keep in touch with others. These pursuits have been linked to improved psychological and emotional health because of their ability to maintain cognitive and social functioning.

Begin a Career in Gardening or Landscaping

Taking care of your own landscaping is a terrific way to keep active and involved if you plan to retire at home or in a community where this is possible. Aside from being a great kind of aerobic exercise, landscaping is also a great method to keep your independence alive and well. For retirees, the advantages of a simple chore like mowing the lawn can last a lifetime. Continuing with the topic of landscaping, nothing makes an outside space look better than a garden you've worked on yourself. Planting flowers or healthy, organic fruits and veggies in a garden is a great way to get some fresh air and exercise, and it also rewards you with the results of your labor.

Balancing Health and Limitations

While it's great that many retirees want to be physically active, it's crucial to take things at your own pace rather than trying to meet someone else's expectations. A wellness plan can include regular exercise, a nutritious diet, and other healthy lifestyle choices, such as playing golf once a week. It's important to establish a plan that you know you can actually follow through on. In spite of their best intentions, many retirees end up spending their days in a similar state of inactivity as before they retired.

It's also never too late to give up harmful behaviors like smoking. Some retirees say they drink more frequently now that they have more free time, so keeping track of your alcohol consumption is another preventative measure you can take to stay healthy in retirement. This is particularly relevant to the aging population that relies on medication.

Maintaining your health and fitness levels does not require a relentless commitment to exercise. It's as simple as paying attention to your body and making an effort to keep it healthy. You'll have to reevaluate your definition of "keeping active" as a result. Just like physical activity, making new connections and engaging in meaningful pursuits can improve one's health. Make sure the retirement community you settle into can assist you in maintaining an active lifestyle.

Chapter 7: Nurturing Your Relationships and Social Connections

The Mental Health Foundation asserts that people who have stronger relationships with their families and friends have greater levels of happiness, enjoy better physical health, and are more likely to live longer. Consequently, whether you plan to spend your retirement doing all of the things you love or exploring new activities, it is essential to remember to keep in touch with your social circle as you start this new chapter in your life. This is especially important if you want to make the most of the time you have in retirement.

It is natural for some friendships to fade away throughout the course of our lives. It may be especially challenging to maintain contact with the people we care about. On the other hand, retirement may present you with the opportunity to invest somewhat more time and energy in the relationships that are most important to you. In addition to this, when limits are loosened, and new vaccines are produced, there will be more opportunities to meet new people and form new friendships. Now that we've established that, let's have a look at some of the methods by which you can continue to maintain and build your social circle during retirement, as well as keep in touch with loved ones while the pandemic is going on.

Building and Maintaining Meaningful Relationships With Friends and Family

While technological advancements have made it simpler to maintain ties and reconnect with old acquaintances, they have also altered our understanding of what constitutes a meaningful friendship. One thousand Facebook friends can make a person feel like a celebrity. But how many of those so-called "friends" would actually stick by them if they went into business for themselves or went through a tough time in their own lives? My experience has taught me that the quality of my connections with my loved ones, acquaintances, and clients directly correlates to the quality of my life overall. The hectic pace of modern life makes it all the more crucial to invest in deep friendships and partnerships.

Find Contentment

Maybe you've heard this one before, but there's a good reason for that: it's still the finest starting point. Peaceful Mind, Peaceful Life author Michelle Maros says it beautifully: "Your relationships outside will flounder if you don't have unconditional love and compassion for yourself."

Train Yourself to Hear and Comprehend

This is an issue that has plagued your life for quite some time. You can blame that on your parents. When it comes to your partner, they never pay attention. Your supervisor either doesn't care or doesn't care to hear you out. According to George P.H.'s Pick The Brain, one of the best ways to connect with others is to listen to them, allow them to finish what they're saying without interjecting, and try to put yourself in their shoes.

Be Optimistic

I have a simple query for you. Who would you prefer to hang out with, a negative person or a positive one? According to Barbara Fredrickson, a psychologist at the University of North Carolina, happy emotions help us "broaden and build" relationships, which is a statement that lends credence to the obvious.

Have a Bite to Eat

Is it really so important for you to eat right now? Most likely, no. Nate Bagley, the resident relationship expert, advises "make the time" to plan a lunch date with a friend, acquaintance, or family member. The payoff for taking this step is substantial.

Make a List of the Connections you Have

Some bonds are meant to endure for decades. Some partnerships are maintained just because they are comfortable and familiar. Think about your connections and decide which ones are worth keeping and which ones are better off being severed. When you let go of toxic relationships, you make room in your life for the ones that are truly meant to be.

Answer the Phone Calls

Sometimes it's nice to communicate by text, email, or Facebook, but nothing beats a face-to-face chat. If you're worried about a friend or peer, don't be too shy to give them a call and see how they're doing. Respecting the other person's time is important, as I've learned. The talk itself need not take up much time. Peter Daisyme, my college roommate, and I do this every day. For the past four years, Peter has worked in a different state from me, but we still talk every day and have closed two business deals together. Pick up the phone or start a Skype session with that pal. It will help a lot in keeping and making connections stronger.

Discover a Shared Passion

It could be a shared interest in a certain sports team, music group, film, line of work, or extreme activity. Finding a shared passion, no matter how big or tiny, is a great way to bond with someone.

Trust Other People

Trusting others is essential, whether or not you have experienced betrayal in the past. To put it clearly, as George P.H. does: "ALL relationships - family, business, platonic - require trust."

Specify your Goals Explicitly

We all hate being let down. But have you ever considered that perhaps you didn't receive what you wanted because you weren't clear about what it was that you needed? Never be afraid to say exactly what you need or want, even if doing so causes you some discomfort.

Get to the Heart of the Question

Steve Boyer has provided us with yet another nugget of wisdom. His theory is that "people will always ask different questions than the one they really want to be answered." To give just one example, "Employees typically ask how to be more successful when all they really want is to get a raise or promotion." What this means is that the answer to the initial query is only the beginning.

Do not Rush Anything

Relationships take time to develop and keep alive. Patience will be a virtue throughout that time as you deal with the inevitable irritations of life. How can you hope to have a long-lasting relationship if you can't put up with the daily hassles that come with being human?

Engage in Direct Gaze

It has long been established through study that "those who make eye contact are viewed as more "likable and trustworthy." The New York Times quotes Dr. Atsushi Senju as saying, "A richer mode of communication is possible right after making eye contact."

Do not Whisper

It's important for couples to talk to each other. Why, then, would you deliberately choose to communicate in ways that are difficult to understand? You may not know this, but mumbling can also be a "sign of covert anger, resentment, disrespect, or sadness."

Laugh

In case you didn't know, humor spreads like wildfire. In addition to improving your health, it can "strengthen our relationships by triggering positive feelings and fostering emotional connection." And don't forget to poke fun at your own foibles every once in a while.

Making New Friends and Social Connections in Retirement

Making new acquaintances becomes more difficult as we age and after retirement, when one of the most usual means to do so is eliminated. According to the founding head of the Stanford Center on Longevity and a psychology professor at Stanford University, baby boomers exhibit the highest indicators of disengaging from traditional ways of social relationships among all age groups.

Pursuing Passions in Retirement

Sharing passions is a powerful bonding factor in friendship. Therefore, if you're looking for buddies in retirement, it's best to seek out others who share your interests.

- Join a group: You might discover a group in your area that shares your interests and values.

- Getting a dog is a great way to meet new people, especially if you and your pet are outgoing. You'll meet more people at the dog park if you establish a regular schedule of visits.

- Volunteer: Having the same goal, like volunteering, can bring individuals closer together.

- Find a Rewarding Part-Time Job: Remember working as a lifeguard when you were younger? Doing college-level wait for service? Putting in a ton of overtime at a new company? If so, you presumably have fond memories of the friends you made there.

- Making friends at work is possible: You need not even go for a physically demanding profession. Find something low-key and enjoyable to do, like working in a nursery or a golf course, and see what kind of people you can meet.

Get Back in Touch with Old Pals

There may be people in your existing network that you enjoy spending time with, but you don't get to see them very often. It could be the perfect time to reconnect with them as true friends. Reach out to them and renew contact. Show them an old photo, catch up on their life, and make some plans!

Spend Time

While friendships may appear to form effortlessly, they need significant time and effort to maintain. According to research conducted by the University of Kansas associate professor of communication studies Jeffrey Hall, it takes between 40 and 60 hours to develop a casual friendship with someone within the first six weeks of knowing them, 80 to 100 hours to develop a casual friend into a friend, and more than 200 hours to develop a friend into a good or best friend. Make sure you set out time every day to cultivate and nurture your friendships. You should talk over the phone, send a note or a small present, and most essential, you should meet in person.

Schedule Recurring Get-Togethers

The regularity of club meetings is a key factor in the success of the socialization they facilitate. If you meet someone you believe you'd get along with, make plans to hang out together on a frequent basis. Anything from going on hikes on Tuesdays and Saturdays to meeting for coffee and supper once a week. Simply keep a consistent schedule of meetings.

You Can Get an App for That! Slide to the Right (or Left)

It's feasible to do so in the real world, but you may find it more convenient to connect with friends online. Did you know there are plenty of apps that aim to help you make friends as well as lovers?

Swiping left indicates disinterest in a possible match while swiping right indicates interest and wanting to communicate.

To help retirees make new friends, here are four helpful websites:

- NextDoor is a social network designed specifically for those living in the same area. People frequently make posts expressing a desire to meet others who share a comparable hobby or pastime.

- In the world of dating apps, Bumble is king. Bumble BFF is their dating service. It's meant to facilitate friendship formation in the same way. Create your own profile with pictures and some text, and then look around at what other people have done.

- Meetup: Meetup is a place to discover and create in-person groups with common interests. Meetup is a social networking service where people may find like-minded people to share experiences and interests. Participate in an existing group, or form your own!

- Friender is an app that finds you local friends that have similar interests.

Persevere

Finding a good buddy is a lot like meeting the love of your life. Trying new people and putting in the time required is essential.

You might have to kiss a few frogs before you find the right friend for you.

Strive to be a Good Friend

- Be a good friend if you desire good friends.

- Sincere, Reliable, and Loyal: The importance of honesty in friendship was highlighted in a global study. 'Disclosing what we're thinking and feeling helps us create trust and closeness,' reports Psychology Today.

- When people are honest with one another, it helps them feel closer to one another and more at ease.

- Giving genuine criticism or taking responsibility for one's actions is a great way to repair strained relationships and keep the peace.

- Kind and Compassionate: Friends deserve our utmost regard and understanding. When one of their friends is in trouble, the other will be there to help.

- Friends crave attention and acknowledgment from their pals. Pose inquiries and take in the responses.

- To be a good friend, you need to be sociable and lighthearted at times, even if you don't feel like it all the time. Keep a positive attitude and a sense of humor.

Ideas for Fun and Social Activities to Enjoy with Others

Finding opportunities for enjoyable and social activities that allow us to interact with people in today's fast-paced and often isolating society can be a challenge. This is often the case after retirement when the structure and regularity of a job no longer provide the same opportunities for interaction with others. Joining a club, doing volunteer work, going on a trip, or just hanging out with friends are all great ways to meet new people and have fun. Here, we'll discuss some possibilities for retirees to have fun and interact with people in a social setting.

Travel

Retirement is the ideal time to travel after working for many years without taking more than a few weeks off at a time. One of the most popular pastimes for retirees is traveling, both domestically and abroad. Vacationing close to home can save you money (especially in light of the current COVID-19 limits on international travel) without sacrificing any of the adventure or novelty of seeing a new place. Traveling to different places and engaging with local customs is an excellent method to broaden one's understanding of the globe. While some travelers have certain destinations in mind, others prefer to keep their itineraries flexible so that they can take in as much of the world as possible. Researching your ideal travel destinations may be an enjoyable and educational hobby, even if international travel is out of the question at the moment.

Giving of One's Time

Volunteering is a great way to rediscover your sense of purpose if you've lost it since leaving the workforce. If you want to feel more content, consider using the abilities you've honed over your life to make a difference in the lives of others in your community. Volunteering has been demonstrated to improve the mental and physical health of older persons, as well as increase their overall sense of fulfillment in life.

Sport

Keeping your body active is crucial to your mental health as well as your physical well-being. Keeping yourself physically active doesn't have to seem like a hassle if you find something you enjoy doing that also provides social opportunities. As long as it gets you up and moving, swimming, surfing, dancing, or even yoga are all fair game. In addition, several sports have groups that meet regularly to help motivate and inspire their members.

Continual Education

The risk of dementia can be mitigated, according to experts, by continuing one's education after retirement. Teaching yourself new skills and learning more about a particular subject can further build your problem-solving skills and increase your general well-being, whether you're preparing to pursue a university degree or just want to get your social media updated. The Tech-Savvy Seniors program and BeConnected both provide free courses for people who want to learn more about technology in order to become more proficient online.

Change your Interests

When you retire, you have the time and freedom to attempt something new. Perhaps you've been so busy with your job and family responsibilities that you've never had much time to pursue a pastime. If you've never had the time before, now might be the perfect time to start a new activity.

You may experiment with new artistic mediums like painting or ceramics, try your hand at a new culinary technique, join a reading club, or even try your hand at growing your own vegetables. Taking up a new hobby is a great way to keep your mind occupied and stave off boredom in retirement, and there are endless options available.

Communities

The good news is that many individuals are in the same position as you, making retirement a wonderful opportunity to discover new friends because of the common experiences you share with them. Feelings of isolation can be mitigated, and emotional support can be drawn upon when one has strong bonds with others. Meeting new people is simple if you join a social club or participate in an organized activity related to a passion or interest you already have. If you're new to the area, it might be challenging to locate such communities, but social media and the local newspaper are excellent resources for learning about upcoming activities. The government in your area might organize special events for retirees.

Chapter 8: Creative Pursuits

Want some fresh ideas about how to spend your free time? Making art can take many forms, such as writing in a diary, playing an instrument, painting, knitting, woodworking, or scrapbooking. Whatever your hobbies or ability levels, there are a wide variety of enjoyable activities that will keep your hands busy and your imagination alive.

Elderly people who engage in artistic pursuits report improvements in motor abilities, social connections, emotional well-being, and stress and anxiety management. Furthermore, creative pursuits have been shown to improve both physical and mental health. There are several ways in which a senior's creative spirit might assist them. Scientists have identified six factors that contribute to healthy aging.

The Benefits of Creativity in Retirement

Because of scientific and medical advancements, people are living longer than ever before. This phenomenon is most pronounced in developed countries. Today's adults maintain their level of physical activity far into their senior years. Adults in their older years are becoming increasingly adventurous and fulfilling their lives with new endeavors.

The topic of how to maximize one's extended lifespan arises as well. Nobody looks forward to becoming older, especially when their health starts to go along with it. That's why a growing number of retirement communities are devoted to enhancing their residents' quality of life.

One method of accomplishing this is through the use of workshops and other creative activities.

Physical and mental well-being can both benefit from engaging in creative pursuits. While art therapy has made great strides in healthcare, its impact on the well-being of the elderly has received less attention. But slowly, governments and experts are beginning to recognize the benefits of arts and crafts for patients. As one might expect, creative pursuits help older people age well by fostering a feeling of purpose, allowing for individual development, and encouraging social interaction. Seniors can gain the motivation and confidence to take charge of their lives through the pursuit of artistic activities such as painting or knitting.

Boost Participation in the Community

Creative workshops have the same positive effects on participants' social lives and sense of community as other forms of community engagement. They can engage in their interest with others in the same room or on their own time, thanks to the workshop format. Seniors who are shy or who have difficulty communicating can nevertheless enjoy artistic activities. It's a great way for people to meet others who share their passions and interests in your community.

Help your Mind

Doing something artistic can help you concentrate better. Trying out new things is a fantastic way to give your mind a healthy workout. The cognitive decline of the elderly can be slowed by engaging in creative activities such as painting, knitting, pottery making, etc.

Art therapy has been shown to improve communication among the elderly. Depression and anxiety relief is another benefit. Artistic and creative pursuits have been demonstrated to be beneficial for people with dementia and Alzheimer's disease.

Start Talking to Strangers

Sharing an interest is a great icebreaker and helps people of all ages bond. However, there are a number of reasons why this is especially crucial for the elderly:

- After retiring, many seniors lose contact with their former workmates.
- They must abandon decades-long friendships in order to move to a senior community.
- They may not see their loved ones too often because of distance.
- Many elderly people experience loneliness because of these reasons. As a result, hosting art workshops for the locals is a great way to get them to meet and connect with others who share their interests.

Improved Physiological Status

There is widespread agreement that an open mind is essential to psychological well-being. However, creative thinking has been linked to improved physical well-being. Engaging in creative pursuits has a calming effect on the nervous system and may reduce stress. Endorphins, neurotransmitters associated with feelings of pleasure and well-being, are also released in response to this.

Find Your Niche in Life and Develop Yourself

A sense of futility is a common reaction to aging. Some of your residents might no longer be working. They are relieved of the responsibilities of parenting and homemaking. They could not be able to or just have no interest in pursuing academic or technical pursuits. Taking up a new creative pursuit might give you the same satisfaction and room for development. They will get better at their art or craft if your residents give it frequent attention and practice. This helps them feel like they're making progress again in their life.

Many working adults and parents have to put their once-cherished pastimes on hold while they advance in their jobs and raise their families. They can't spare the time right now. In-house art classes provide residents the opportunity to pick up where they left off, however long ago that may have been. There is a wide variety of imaginative pursuits you could introduce to your inhabitants. Contrary to popular belief, they are not confined to the visual arts. You could host a reading club, a creative writing group, a pottery class, a knitting group, a quilting group, a sewing group, a collage-making group, etc. Some of these pursuits may even lend themselves to regular club meetings, depending on interest and attendance.

Exploring Creative Pursuits in Retirement

It's common to put off creative projects and leisure activities until retirement, but that doesn't mean you can't finally get around to them. Participating in these kinds of things can make you happy, keep your brain engaged, and introduce you to new people. There are various ways to indulge your artistic interests, whether you have a penchant for writing, painting, photography, ceramics, sewing, music, cuisine, or jewelry creation. Classes, organizations, courses, and even just experimenting on your own are all viable options. Trying out new things like these is a great way to exercise your imagination, pick up useful skills, and live a more fulfilling life.

Photography

Many retirees find that their time spent photographing the world around them is a rewarding creative outlet. Retirees have more time on their hands and more opportunities to travel, both of which lend themselves well to the pursuit of photography. The ability to set goals and strive towards developing one's skills through photography can also give retirees a feeling of purpose and direction in life. Photographers in retirement can take advantage of a variety of educational opportunities to hone their craft. They can also join photography organizations and groups to meet like-minded people, exhibit their work, and get critiques. Photography is a popular pastime among retirees because it encourages mindfulness and a sense of gratitude for the world around you.

Taking up photography as a retirement hobby allows you to see the world in a different, more artistic light. Photography is a great hobby for retirees, who can utilize their skills to record their travels, capture the natural world, or simply record their daily lives. Retirees can keep growing as photographers and reaping the advantages of self-expression by trying out new approaches and approaches to familiar subjects. In general, photography is a great hobby for retirees to have. It allows retirees to document and share their experiences with others while also providing possibilities for creativity, socialization, and personal improvement. There's no better time than retirement to go headfirst into photography, whether you're a seasoned pro or just getting your feet wet.

Gardening

two elderly ladies gardening togetherIncorporating gardening into your outdoor activity and social schedule is a win-win. Get your hands dirty, plant some seeds, tend to them, and then harvest your hard work. Beautiful plants and crisp vegetables could be just the thing to help you unwind. Moreover, this activity provides a welcome opportunity to obtain some much-needed exercise and Vitamin D. You can use your imagination while designing a garden's layout to maximize productivity and aesthetic value throughout the summer.

Coloring Pages & Painting Activities

Markers and paintbrushes are popular tools for self-expression among many people. Taking in a scene with soothing patterns and colors is like giving your brain a break from the stresses of the day. Coloring has been demonstrated to have a soothing effect on the body, similar to that of meditation. So, have a look at these paintings and drawings for inspiration:

Adult coloring books prove that drawing is fun for people of all ages. Coloring books for adults are gaining popularity as a therapeutic and artistic outlet for people of all ages. Coloring books with large fonts are available for adults who have trouble seeing the page. Geometric tape painting entails taping off a grid of lines on a canvas, painting inside the lines, and then removing the tape. This is a great way for seniors with shaky hands to paint a masterpiece with clean, even strokes.

Learn More About Mindfulness and Meditation

Two seniors sit in nature and meditate. The benefits of mindfulness meditation are numerous, ranging from improved mental health (less stress, less worry) to physical health (less inflammation, less cortisol). This form of meditation has been shown to improve mental wellness and creativity. It's easier to come up with original concepts when you're relaxed and free of mental clutter. Mindfulness meditation helps you train your attention so that you can observe your inner experiences—your thoughts, feelings, and bodily functions—without interference. The seed of that novel you've always wanted to write could be lurking in these unfiltered ideas. Just try it out and see what happens.

Put on a Show

Two forms of musical self-expression include singing along with your favorite songs and playing an instrument. Get lost in some tunes and see what happens, whether it's a flood of nostalgia or the want to try out some new moves.

Get Started Keeping a Journal

Writing about one's experiences is a common way for the elderly to pass on their wisdom to the next generation. Keeping a journal, however, has several benefits beyond that memory preservation. Writing has been linked to numerous health advantages, including increased brain power and reduced anxiety. For many, the hardest part of writing is getting started and overcoming writer's block. Just start writing and see what occurs. You can find formal writing prompts online to jumpstart your imagination.

Creating a Website or Novel

The publishing industry is far more flexible now than it was a century ago, giving you many options. Why not start a blog instead? When it comes to telling your life story or cooking up your favorite dish, the only limit is your creativity. The added bonus of making a simple website is that it forces you to exercise your imagination. You don't need to be technologically savvy to make a simple website using platforms like Wix or WordPress.

If that doesn't sound fun, maybe you might try writing a novel instead. If you're feeling overwhelmed, try reading a few short stories or recounting some personal experiences. This undertaking can be widely disseminated via the internet or in print form thanks to the ease with which one can now self-publish one's work. Try your luck!

Participate in a Book Group

If you're a reader, you probably love having the opportunity to talk about the books you've read with others. Book clubs have a dual purpose of keeping members socially engaged and intellectually active. If you're looking for like-minded people, look in your local area or consider joining a virtual book club.

Volunteer

Engage in acts of kindness. You can still make a difference in your neighborhood, even if you are bedridden or have limited mobility. This is a great way to keep busy and gain satisfaction from your efforts. Investigate local non-profits to see if there are any opportunities to lend a hand. Assisting with the assembly of care packages, knitting or crocheting blankets or hats, or making blankets are all examples.

Chapter 9: Enjoying Nature and the Outdoors

When you retire, you finally have the time to appreciate the outdoors. More leisure time means more opportunities to visit parks and nature preserves, join new groups, pursue exciting pursuits, organize road trips and much more. If you want to deepen your connection with nature, try taking up a hobby like bird watching, fishing, or gardening. Wearing sunscreen and protective gear, staying hydrated, and taking breaks when necessary are all essential for maintaining good health as you age. Having fun and appreciating nature's splendor are the top priorities. Get your boots dirty, and go discover the world!

The Benefits of Spending Time in Nature

One of the best ways to unwind and recharge is to spend time outdoors, taking in the sights and sounds of nature. Numerous medical experts now advocate for patients to spend more time outdoors. The elderly would especially profit from taking walks in parks, taking deep breaths of fresh air, and basking in the sun.

Vitamin D3 Boost

Vitamin D is a crucial immune system supplement. Sunlight exposure results in the synthesis of this vitamin. Spending as much time as possible, outside has health benefits, especially for the elderly. Strong bones require calcium, which is best absorbed with the help of vitamin D. It's also important for immunity, as it aids the body's defenses against illness and infection. It helps the body make antibodies that can neutralize viruses before they can do any harm. In order to increase their vitamin D levels, the members of our team advocate for seniors to spend more time outside.

Boosts Defense Mechanisms

Research suggests that contact with nature can boost the immune system. Spending more time outside with our loved ones encourages physical activity, which in turn boosts their immune systems by increasing blood flow and decreasing their susceptibility to illness.

Take in Some Clean Air

Getting your loved ones outside more allows them to take in some clean air. Do you realize that breathing in clean air can greatly improve our well-being? The simple act of going outside and letting some fresh air in can do wonders for your respiratory system, your immune system, your blood pressure, and your digestion. It can also revitalize our loved ones, boosting their concentration and general well-being.

Spend Time in Nature

When seniors spend more time outside, they gain so much more than just the health benefits associated with natural light and air. The healing effects of spending time outdoors with our loved ones include but are not limited to the simple acts of taking in the sights, sounds, and smells of nature.

Calms Nervousness and Depressive Symptoms

There is mounting evidence that exposing elderly people to nature might help them feel better emotionally. Your loved ones will feel less confined, which will help you achieve your goal. It's hard to be concerned about anything when you're surrounded by such beautiful nature. The stunning scenery may inspire you to get out of your camera. Clearly, nothing beats a day at the park, surrounded by loved ones, as a form of therapy and health maintenance for the elderly. There would be a variety of senior living communities in Shelby to choose from if you or an aging loved one is thinking about making the transition.

Outdoor Activities in Retirement

Hiking

Hiking is a wonderful way to get some exercise and see the outdoors. In regional parks, national parks, and forests, you can go hiking on well-kept trails. Hiking routes range in difficulty; pick one that's appropriate for your level of fitness. In addition to packing lots of water and snacks, you should wear comfortable, durable shoes for the journey. In case of an emergency, make sure to let someone know where you're going and pack a map and compass.

Camping

When you go camping, you can relax and appreciate nature without any distractions. You can stay in a cabin, tent, or RV. Pick a campground that provides the basics, like hot showers and flush toilets. Follow the Leave No Trace principles when camping, which include removing any waste, showing consideration for wildlife, and returning the site to its original state.

Birdwatching

Birdwatching is a common pastime among people who value the outdoors. Birds can be seen in the wild in places like forests, marshes, and parks. Obtaining quality binoculars and a bird identification reference are essential first steps. Consider signing up with a local birdwatching club, where you may pick the brains of seasoned watchers and discover uncharted territory.

Fishing

You can enjoy some quiet time by yourself or with a group of friends while fishing. Lakes, rivers, and oceans are all excellent fishing spots. Make sure you are in compliance with all licensing and permit requirements set forth by your municipality. To keep the fish population healthy, anglers should practice catch-and-release techniques.

Biking

Biking is a fun and healthy way to see the world around you. Biking is possible on paved roads, dirt paths, and even in the highlands. Put money on a high-quality bicycle and safety gear like a helmet and reflective clothing. You should also know the regulations of the road when riding a bike, such as riding only on bike lanes and always using reflective gear.

Kayaking/Canoeing

Those who like being on the water can't go wrong with kayaking or canoeing. You can use a kayak on any body of water, from a pond to the ocean. Purchase a high-quality kayak or canoe, as well as essential safety gear like a life jacket. Learn the water safety guidelines, such as always wearing a life vest and keeping an eye on the forecast.

Gardening

Having a garden allows you to get in touch with nature while also providing you with fresh produce. Plant some flowers or some vegetables. Select vegetation suitable to your region's weather and soil conditions. Stress and anxiety can be reduced via gardening as well.

Geocaching

Geocaching is an outdoor version of the classic treasure hunt. Geocaching is a worldwide treasure-hunting activity in which participants use GPS receivers to locate concealed containers. It's a fun way to test your limits and discover something new. Geocaching websites and apps can help you locate caches in your immediate region.

Ascents of Rocks

Rock climbing is a difficult sport that calls for physical prowess and technical know-how. Both indoor and outdoor climbing is possible. Climbing shoes, a harness, and a helmet are all essential pieces of equipment. You should also learn the correct methods and safety standards for rock climbing by enrolling in a program or employing a guide.

Taking to the Saddle

Riding horses is a great way to spend time by yourself or with a group of friends. Parks, woodlands, and the seashore are all viable options for riding. A sturdy set of riding boots and a helmet are essential safety accessories. Learn the fundamentals and safety precautions for horseback riding with a class or guided trail ride.

In general, doing things outside is a wonderful way to both appreciate nature and stay physically active. They can also be a fun method to meet individuals with similar interests. To have a good time and stay safe, you should always plan ahead and observe safety procedures.

BONUS 1: Practical Advice on Planning for Retirement

Financial Planning

Pressure on public pension systems in developed countries has increased as their population ages, making it more important than ever for individuals to save for their own retirements. The negative effects of a lack of preparedness have made Retirement Financial preparedness (RFP) a necessity. However, FPR is difficult for a number of reasons, including a lack of information, individual considerations, and fear of dying.

The Importance of Retirement Planning in Developed Nations

Without private pensions and personal retirement savings, society cannot ensure a decent standard of living in old age. Due to the high, intermediate, and long-term detrimental consequences of bad planning, governments have developed increasingly aggressive measures meant to involve citizens in FPR.

The Complicated Nature of Retirement Budgeting

Lack of information, individual differences, and the emotional strain of thinking about death all contribute to the difficulty of FPR.

Theoretical Frameworks for Retirement Income Management

The field of economics has found that the field of psychology provides useful concepts for understanding economic behavior, and the field of psychology has recognized the significance of retirement savings. Without a theoretical model or with more comprehensive models like the Theory of Reasoned Action, empirical research on FPR has increased.

The Ability-Desire-Chance Hypothesis

The "Capacity-Willingness-Opportunity Model" was presented to explain FPR by Hershey, Jacobs-Lawson, and Austin in 2013. The model incorporates a time component and examines age and stage in addition to their interaction with the other aspects of the model; it is particular, comprehensive, and procedural.

The Capability, Willingness, and Opportunity Triadic Model

The Capacity-Willingness-Opportunity Model takes into account these three factors in retirement preparation: capability, willingness, and opportunity. Willingness consists of the motivational factors that drive planning activities and saving, while capacity refers to the mental characteristics and abilities necessary to plan and save for retirement. Last but not least, the opportunity dimension recognizes the impact of environmental facilitators and restrictions on efficient financial tasking.

Capacity, Willingness, and Opportunity as a Procedural Model

The model is procedural and relies on the premise that one's FPR will remain stable and grow stronger as one gets older. Hershey's approach includes a sophisticated age component.

Age's Impact on the Availability of Resources and Opportunities

In the Capability-Willingness-Opportunity Model, age plays a nuanced role. Under the continuity hypothesis, one would anticipate the capacity, willingness, and chances to plan and save to remain relatively constant over time. However, there are at least three sorts of impacts that could contribute to shifts in FPR: typical age-related influences, typical historical influences, and out-of-the-ordinary life occurrences.

Support for the Capability-Willingness-Opportunity Model from Real-World Data

The Capacity-Willingness-Opportunity Model still has limited and inconsistent empirical support. Although there is a large body of empirical work spanning more than a decade that tests parts of the model, no work has yet tested the full model.

Planning for Retirement Based on Intentional Change Theory

According to Intentional Change Theory (ICT), the formulation of a personal vision or dream is the starting point for every journey toward lasting, intended change. ICT also relies heavily on the kind of meaningful, trustworthy connections that give people the freedom to pursue their dreams and keep them alive. A desirable mental picture of old age and a sound financial strategy for retirement can be greatly aided by the assistance of coaches or trustworthy consultants.

Creating a Retirement Plan

It's important to think about the things that will influence your retirement plans as soon as possible. What are your upcoming plans for the family? Having children is a major life goal for many individuals, but it can also significantly reduce your financial security. Therefore, your retirement strategy should take into account your desired family composition.

Similar consideration should be given to where you intend to live in retirement if you have any such intentions. Extensive travel during retirement, as many people imagine doing, can be a great adventure but can also quickly deplete a retiree's savings. Moving to a country with a low cost of living, on the other hand, could help you make your money go further while still providing a comfortable level of living. Self-funded plans, such as 401(k) or IRA accounts, have essentially supplanted pension funds as the standard for skilled professionals. Your retirement plan should take into account the various tax-advantaged accounts you can open, each of which has its own maximum contribution limit.

The following are the next steps in retirement planning after you have given this some thought:

Know How Far Ahead You Need to Plan

The foundation for a successful retirement plan is your current age and your projected retirement age. You can take on more risk in your portfolio the further away from retirement you are. With 30 years or more until retirement, a young person can afford to put the bulk of their savings into riskier investments like equities. The stock market will experience volatility, but over the long term, equities have typically outperformed other securities like bonds. The key word here is "long," which indicates a time period of at least 10 years.

To keep your purchasing power in retirement, you need returns that are higher than inflation. Acorn inflation is what we have now. Financial planner Chris Hammond of Savannah, Tennessee, and creator of RetirementPlanningMadeEasy.com, compares the process to planting a seed that, with time and care, can grow into a towering oak tree. We've all heard of and ideally strive for compound growth in our investments, Hammond chimes in. "Well, inflation is like 'compound anti-growth since it gradually destroys the purchasing power of your money. In about 24 years, the value of your investments will have decreased by half due to an apparently insignificant 3% inflation rate. Doesn't seem like much every year, but over time it adds up to a significant change.

You should prioritize income and capital preservation in your portfolio as you become older. This means putting more of your money into safer investments like bonds, which won't generate as much income as stocks but are less likely to lose value. You'll worry about inflation less as a result, too. Cost-of-living increases are less of a concern for a 64-year-old who will retire the following year than they are for a much younger professional who has just entered the field.

Your retirement plan should have several parts. Take the example of a couple of planning to retire in two years, fund their child's college tuition till they're 18, and then relocate to Florida. A retirement plan would divide the investment strategy into three time periods: the two years before retirement (during which contributions are still made to the plan), the time spent saving for and paying for education, and the time spent living in Florida (during which regular withdrawals are made to fund living expenses).

The ideal allocation method for a multi-stage retirement plan should take into account participants' time horizons and liquidity demands at each stage. As your investment horizon shifts over time, your portfolio should undergo periodic rebalancing. While it may not seem like much now, those small savings in your twenties will add up to a significant sum by the time you actually need the money.

Calculate Your Annual Retirement Costs

The size of a retirement portfolio can be estimated with the support of realistic expectations about spending patterns in retirement. The common assumption is that once retired, one's annual spending will be somewhere between 70% and 80% of what it was before retirement. This is usually not the case, especially if the mortgage has not been paid off or if unexpected medical bills have to be paid. Adults often use their first few years of retirement to treat themselves to trips and other once-in-a-lifetime experiences.

The cost of living, notably medical care, continues to rise every year. With a higher life expectancy comes the desire to enjoy one's golden years. Adults in retirement require a higher standard of living for a longer period of time; necessitating increased savings and investment efforts. Since retirees don't have to spend eight or more hours a day working, they have more disposable income to spend on vacations, sightseeing, and retail therapy. More spending in retirement requires more savings now, so having an accurate target helps with planning.

Your withdrawal rate is a major determinant of how long your retirement savings will last. The amount you withdraw annually and how you invest in your account are both heavily influenced by your estimate of retirement needs. Kevin Michels, CFP, EA, president of Medicus Wealth Planning in Draper, Utah, warns that it's easy to outlive your portfolio if you underestimate your retirement needs, and it's risky to overestimate your retirement income if you don't want to sacrifice the lifestyle you desire in old age.

Planning for retirement requires thinking about your life expectancy so that you don't outlive your money. Humans are living longer than ever before. Individuals and couples can calculate their longevity risk with the help of actuarial life tables. If you plan to buy a house or pay for your children's college education after you retire, you may need more money than you anticipate. These costs should be included in the total retirement budget. Make sure you are still on track with your savings by revising your plan annually. "Specifying and estimating early retirement activities," "accounting for unexpected expenses in middle retirement," and "forecasting what-if late retirement medical costs" are all ways to increase the precision of retirement planning, as explained by Alex Whitehouse, AIF, CRPC, CWS, president and CEO of Whitehouse Wealth Management in Vancouver, Washington.

Determine the Effective Rate of Return on Investments

Once the investment horizon and expenditure needs have been established, the real after-tax rate of return may be computed to evaluate the portfolio's potential to generate the required income. Even for long-term investments, it is impossible to expect a rate of return of more than 10% (before taxes). This is because low-risk retirement portfolios are typically made up of low-yielding fixed-income securities, which means the required rate of return decreases as you become older.

Assuming no taxes and the maintenance of the portfolio balance, an individual with a $400,000 retirement account and income needs of $50,000 would require an unreasonable 12.5% return. When you start saving for retirement early on, your portfolio has more time to grow and protect your desired rate of return. A more reasonable predicted return of 5% would be achieved with a $1,000,000 gross retirement investment account.

Investment returns are normally taxed depending on the sort of retirement account you possess. The after-tax rate of return is what matters in determining the true rate of return. One of the most important steps in retirement preparation is figuring out how you'll be taxed once you start taking money out of your retirement account.

Compare Investment Objectives to Risk Tolerance

An appropriate portfolio allocation that balances the worries of risk aversion and returns targets is likely the most crucial phase in retirement planning, whether you are making the investment decisions yourself or hiring a professional money manager. In order to achieve your goals, how much are you ready to risk? Should I invest a portion of my income in safe Treasury bonds in covering my fixed costs?

"If you are investing money you won't need to touch for 40 years, you can afford to see your portfolio value rise and fall with those cycles," says John R. Frye, CFA, senior advisor at Carnegie Investment Counsel. Don't sell when the market drops; instead, purchase. Don't give in to a state of terror. You would want to take advantage of a 20% off deal on shirts, right? I mean, if equities went on sale at 20% off, why not?" Amounting to $12.06 million, The value of an estate that can be passed on tax-free in the United States in 2022. Estate taxes are paid on amounts over that threshold.

Keep Up-to-Date with Your Estate Plan

An effective retirement strategy should also include careful estate planning, which calls for the assistance of specialized specialists such as lawyers and accountants. In addition to an estate plan and retirement preparations, life insurance is an essential financial asset. If you want to make sure your loved ones are taken care of financially after your death, you need to have both a solid estate plan and adequate life insurance. A well-thought-out strategy can also help you avoid the time-consuming and costly probate process.

Estate planning includes thinking about how your assets will be taxed. The tax consequences of giving versus leaving assets through an estate must be weighed if individual plans to leave assets to loved ones or a nonprofit organization. One frequent method of investing for retirement is to aim for returns high enough to cover annual living expenditures after adjusting for inflation. The deceased person's heirs or beneficiaries receive the portfolio. A tax expert should be consulted in order to ascertain the best course of action.

"Estate planning will vary over an investor's lifetime," says Mark T. Hebner, president and founder of Index Fund Advisors Inc. in Irvine, California, and author of Index Funds: The 12-Step Recovery Program for Active Investors. "Essential legal documents like powers of attorney and wills should be drawn out right away. After starting a family, a trust may become an integral part of your long-term financial strategy. When it comes to taxes and fees, Hebner says, "How you would like your money dispersed will be of the utmost importance later in life." The preparation and maintenance of this part of your financial plan might be facilitated by working with a fee-only estate planning attorney.

Setting Goals

The following are some things to consider when mapping for your retirement:

Make it Easy

The simplest strategies often prove to be the most effective. Simplifying your plans for retirement entails making use of any employer-provided retirement savings plan, like a 401(k). Consider creating a Roth IRA if your company does not provide a retirement plan. Set up automatic contributions into your retirement plan of choice to keep yourself on track to retire when you want to.

Calculating Retirement Savings

Many financial experts recommend setting aside 15 percent of one's annual salary for retirement. You can achieve this rate by keeping a spending diary for a month and noting where you have spare cash. You should invest this in your retirement. Determine an alternative maximum amount and establish a plan that permits you to climb to 15% of your yearly gross income every year if you are unable to save 15% of your annual gross income for retirement. For instance, you may start at 5% and work your way up to 15%.

Realize How Much Time There Is to Put Money Away for Retirement

When planning for retirement, it's crucial to take into account your time horizon or the number of years until you plan to retire officially. You can make riskier investments with a higher return potential if you have a longer time horizon. Start saving for retirement later in life? Consider safer investments that yield more stable returns.

Knowing How Much Money You'll Need

The best way to prepare for retirement is to be realistic about how much money you expect to spend once you stop working. If you plan to do a lot of traveling after you retire, for instance, you might want to save up a special traveling fund in addition to your regular retirement savings. Other factors to think about are:

Put Money Down for the Future

When planning for retirement, many people look to investing for financial security. Investing for the long run, rather than the short term, is preferable when saving for retirement. If you plan to put money into the stock market, this is especially true. Consider working with a financial adviser if you need help deciding where to put your money.

Recognize The Need

If you're just starting to save for retirement, you might want to take some calculated risks in order to see your nest egg increase as quickly as possible. Since you may need access to your investment funds as you age, reevaluating your strategy and minimizing exposure to risk is prudent. Certificates of deposit, for instance, offer higher interest rates than many conventional savings accounts and carry very little risk.

Bonus 2: Traveling on a Budget

Tips for Affordable and Sustainable Travel

We can all agree that seeing the world is a life-changing and self-actualizing experience. You get exposed to different ways of life, eating, and doing things. Your horizons will broaden, and your mind will open the more you travel. However, modern travel needs greener modes of transportation. As budget-minded globetrotters, we need to adopt more environmentally friendly practices and reduce our environmental impact. One of the things pressing us now is climate change, which brings with it hotter weather, more frequent and intense wildfires, higher sea levels, and thawing glaciers. According to the research, tourism accounts for 8% of all global emissions of greenhouse gases. Two to three tons of carbon dioxide are released by each person on a round trip from Europe to the United States. That's a major deal!

Therefore, it is evident that we must develop greener travel habits. But how do you achieve this while still keeping your travel expenses low? Check out the advice below to learn how to plan a trip that won't have a negative impact on the environment.

Pack Minimally

Packing less clothing is a great way to lighten your load and help the environment. Having extra toiletries, pairs of shoes, or garments on hand is a common "just in case" justification for overpacking. We incur more costs due to excess baggage and often choose environmentally harmful modes of transportation. If your bags aren't too heavy, you can transport them by yourself. You can take the bus or a cab, whatever you like. Less stuff to lug along means more freedom to do what you want to do.

Limit Your Air Travel

Avoiding airplanes as much as possible is recommended because they are a major source of air pollution. There will be times when that is unavoidable, and in those cases, the best option is to go with a cheap business. Cheap flights may be crowded and may not offer much legroom, but they are preferable to first class. First-class passengers do have more room, but they also tend to eat more alcohol and food. Remember that everyone is going to the same place, so you might be able to put up with the annoyances of flying with a budget airline.

If you can help it, limit your use of airplanes. It's obvious why most people keep using it nevertheless, as it is the quickest mode of transportation. You can take the bus or the train if you're not in a hurry and have lots of time. Because they are on a schedule and making frequent journeys, they are able to reduce their environmental impact. They're more cost-effective than cars; therefore, you should definitely go that route.

Go Out and Ride a Bike or Walk

Avoid driving or taking a cab if the distance is less than a few miles. Rent a bike or just go for a walk; they are both better alternatives than driving.

If the weather isn't conducive to walking, you always have the option of taking public transportation.

If you're visiting a country with a well-developed cycling infrastructure, renting a bike may be the best option. Both the Netherlands and Denmark are examples. Biking is beneficial to your health in many ways. It's good for your heart and lungs, your muscles, and your joints. And because it produces no pollution, it is a sustainable mode of transportation, especially for short trips. Similar health benefits are associated with walking. The risk of cardiovascular disease and stroke are both decreased as a result. It's a green and healthy option for getting about town.

Increase Your Length of Stay at Each Location

The longer you stay in one place, the less gas you use getting there and back and the less trash you produce. If you want to see additional sites and nations throughout your vacation, regardless of the mode of transportation you choose, you should strive to arrange it in a different way. Try not to hop around from place to place, staying for only a day or two at each. Instead, try to extend your stay. Learn the lay of the land and locate less-trodden attractions with this method.

Staying for a longer period of time can also help you save money on lodging. Spending more time in one location might be beneficial since it allows one to become acclimated to the norms of that location. You completely submerge yourself in their way of life, giving you the best possible chance of picking up some fascinating and useful new routines.

This is great advice for frugal travelers who want to avoid spending a lot of money on commuting between locations. Additionally, your actions and mode of transportation are more eco-friendly.

Eco-Friendly Hostels Are Better Than Hotels

It is not more expensive to stay at an eco-friendly establishment than at a conventional one. This method can reduce CO_2 emissions by as much as 8 kg per person every night. Everything from the electricity to the cleaning supplies to the food to the garbage is guaranteed to be eco-friendly and well-sorted.

- Go for eco-friendly hostels or any place where you can stay in a shared room with other travelers. To begin, staying in a shared dorm room is a great way to cut costs. Hotel rooms are unnecessary unless you need to use them to prepare for a presentation or attend an essential event. More power and energy are required to make them cozy and inviting.

- Second, you can meet friendly locals who are eager to share their culture with you. Why not take advantage of the chance to meet new people and do your part for the environment at the same time?

- Third, when on the road, it's important to realize that you'll just be using your hotel room to sleep. If you plan on seeing the sights during the day, a hostel is a great option for a cost-effective and environmentally friendly overnight stay.

Consider House-Sitting

While traveling on a tight budget, there is still a way to lessen your negative effects on the planet. There are increasingly more people who require the services of a house sitter. Some of them are trying to find house sitters who are willing to take care of their dogs while they are away. Therefore, home-sitting is an option for you if you enjoy taking care of animals. Home maintenance typically entails looking after things like plants and animals. Since throwing parties is prohibited, this may be your best option for a place to stay. You may save some cash this way and still have time to see the sights in the city.

Opt for Neighborhood Eateries

A hostel is more likely to have a kitchen than a hotel. To show your support for the community, you can choose to shop at local markets for your ingredients. There is no easy way to determine how much your dinner contributed to greenhouse gas emissions, but you should know that meals using imported products have a larger carbon footprint.

If your lodging provides a kitchen, you can prepare your own meals. Purchasing ready-to-eat meals from a grocery store chain is the simplest option. Buying them in bulk at a grocery store can save you a lot of money compared to eating out. Although restaurant fare is likely to be of higher quality, you can find a variety of tasty options at the supermarket. In addition, the cuisine available there is excellent.

Don't Use Disposable Utensils and Plates

Or, better yet, don't use any plastics that can't be reused. About half of all plastic made each year is destined for single use. Because of the low recycling rates in many nations, annually, approximately 8 million tons of plastic are added to the world's oceans. The best option is to invest in durable bamboo flatware and eating utensils that can be used over and over again. Metal straws and flatware can also be purchased at a discount on the web. You may save money and reduce your carbon footprint by using them.

Best Destinations and Accommodations for Budget Travel

Vacations are fun, but they can be pricey. Inflation affects many bottom lines, making it easy to allow a concern of increased prices to deter you from scheduling your next trip. Americans value travel. The U.S. Travel Association travel spending this year will exceed pre-pandemic levels. While demand is strong and steals and discounts difficult to find (you should know the optimum time to book a flight and a hotel), there are plenty of affordable destinations to explore across the world and terrific travel apps to help you plan.

We have the best budget-friendly short vacations and huge adventures in the U.S. and throughout the world. These places provide inexpensive vacations without sacrificing leisure or fun. Outside of peak seasons, when airfare and accommodation prices drop, all are excellent. Avoid June through August in Europe for the cheapest trip and to satisfy your wanderlust.

Lisbon (Europe)

Portugal has Europe's biggest hits at affordable prices. Lisbon, its capital, is rated in Kayak's top 10 travel trends report for its cheap international airline (average $708 round trip) and $153 nightly hotel rates. You don't need money to have fun here. Walk Lisbon's winding, scenic cobblestone streets packed with stores, restaurants, fountains, and monuments of leaders and poets. Try a pastel de nata (egg custard dessert) for 1 euro from a bakery or a shot of ginja, the Portuguese cherry liquor, in a little chocolate cup for 1.20 euros at one of the many vendors. The Tasca do Chico in town offers authentic and cheap Fado performances.

Colombia, Cartagena

Cartagena, Colombia, the most romantic city in the country, is a tropical paradise on the Caribbean coast. New York is five hours away, and Miami is three. (No big international airport near you? Consider pricing out a supplemental ticket that gets you to your primary flight's location.) Airfare is normally mid-$500 round trip, and Kayak's inexpensive hotels are $182 per night.

With colorful castles, cobblestone lanes, and colonial churches, the capital city is a World Heritage Site. The low cost of living in a country with many first-world facilities and infrastructure makes this city one of the cheapest locations to vacation. Enjoy $4 multi-course dinners and 25-cent coffee. Try an arepa con queso, too. Need a Colombian vacation read? Gabriel García Márquez set The Love in the Time of Cholera and Of Love and Other Demons in Cartagena.

Ohio's Mason

For kids! The Midwest has some of the most thrilling theme parks for budget family trips. Ohio is one of the cheapest U.S. tourist destinations and a lot of fun. Its Midwestern location makes it one of America's best road excursions. Family Destinations Guide found Kings Island in Mason, Ohio, to be the greatest bargain for accommodation, tickets, food, and general expenses. It's the cheapest day out for a family of four compared to other big U.S. amusement parks, with the lowest daily food spend ($26.32), park ticket average ($160), and lodging average ($79). Want a week? Cedar Point, Ohio, a three-hour trip from Mason, came in second with $180 per day for a family of four.

Mexico City (North America)

This North American city is a good value among Mexico's many tourist spots. Mexico City has many world-class museums and art institutes with low admission rates. The exchange rate exceeds 18 pesos per dollar. Looking for top Mexican all-inclusive resorts? All-inclusive housing in Mexico may be affordable because it includes meals, drinks, and activities. Mexico City has affordable hotels and flights for Airbnb and regular hotels. Save money!

Prague (Europe)

We love Prague, one of Europe's most charming and affordable ancient cities. Bright red trams ($1.35) travel cobblestone streets flanked by lovely stone buildings in the excellently preserved city. Every corner has a free attraction, like the classic taverns (grab a pilsner pint for $2) or the medieval Charles Bridge with its imposing stone statues. Another highlight: Prague Castle is surrounded by a castle area. Not only the Prague city center offers cheap entertainment. Visit beautiful wineries in the countryside on a budget. We also guarantee economical luxury in big and small hotels.

Uruguay, Colonia del Sacramento

Uruguay, a South American jewel, is close to Buenos Aires but more laid-back. Americans visiting Uruguay will get good value for their money due to the 26-to-1 exchange rate. History aficionados can enjoy 17th, 18th, and 19th-century relics in Colonia del Sacramento. The city's World Heritage-listed cobbled streets, lined with colorful residences, cafés, and stores, provide historic walking tours. Block parties in summer serve authentic Uruguayan street food. Even eating out all day can cost less than $10.

Small boutiques cost $50 per night, whereas Sheraton hotels cost $160. Round-trip flights average $540. Since the country is in the Southern Hemisphere, its summer high season is December through February, making it one of the top winter tourism locations. November and March offer the finest discounts and weather.

Puerto Rico, San Juan

Puerto Rico is easy and cheaper than you think. You don't need a passport, customs, or money to visit this gorgeous tropical island in the

US. The greatest all-inclusive resorts offer cheap entertainment once you arrive. Puerto Rico, especially San Juan, is one of the greatest U.S. destinations for cheap beach vacations. Visit Old San Juan and Castillo San Felipe del Morro, a 16th–18th-century citadel. Try a tripleta, a Puerto Rican sandwich with marinated meats that costs $8 at a food truck, for lunch.

We've seen East Coast round-trip flights for under $200, but using points or credit card travel incentives to go to Puerto Rico can be extremely useful. Winter and spring break hotels cost the most. Hurricane season makes late summer and early fall unsuitable. The remainder of the year has gorgeous weather.

Asia: Bangkok

Visit Thailand, one of the world's most underestimated locations. This unforgettable Southeast Asian vacation in the Land of Smiles offers peaceful, adventurous, culinary, and cultural experiences at an affordable price. Bangkok is the cheapest travel destination. In a luxury-on-a-budget survey by money.co.uk, Bangkok was the cheapest city in the world for luxury car rentals, Michelin-starred meals, and five-star hotel stays, with the cheapest luxury hotels starting at $110. In late spring, flights from the East Coast cost $860 round way (avoid midsummer). Travelers can enjoy authentic Thai spas ($10 an hour), delicious local cuisine, and a tuk-tuk ride ($1.50) to see the golden temples along the Chao Phraya River.

Toronto, Canada

Many vacationers may easily visit Toronto, one of Canada's most popular destinations, in 90 minutes from 60% of the US. Since the U.S. dollar is strong versus the Canadian dollar, the city will feel like a sale. According to Kayak, Toronto has some of the best hotel and flight prices, with overnight accommodations costing $202 and round-trip travel $375.

Visit the top of the CN Tower for stunning views. Ride the moving sidewalk through a shark tank at Ripley's aquarium next door. The $56 Toronto CityPASS offers cheap entrance to five renowned attractions, including both. Toronto's most popular free attraction—Lake Ontario's downtown beaches—is best enjoyed in the summer. Family-friendly summer sun.

Cape Town, South Africa

South Africa is a bucket list destination and one of the finest vacation destinations in 2023. Is it affordable? We agree! If traveling to South Africa sounded too expensive, reconsider. Delta and United have inaugurated non-stop flights to the country, creating competition on the routes and lowering costs, especially in late spring and late fall, when rates drop well below $900 round trip. Most motels cost $100 or less due to the conversion rate of roughly 18 rand to the dollar. Every budget can afford gourmet restaurants and award-winning wines.

Table Mountain overlooks Cape Town. Explore Robben Island's complex history. Explore the Cape Town Winelands, famous for its vineyards, scenery, and history. Visit Cape Point to witness African penguins, zebra, and other animals.

Guatemala, Antigua

Antigua, Guatemala—not the Caribbean island—is Central America's next hip city. The Pacaya volcano surrounds this colonial village. A half-day volcano walking trip with a native guide, park entry, a water bottle, and hotel transportation costs $22. Travelers who bring marshmallows and skewers can toast them with the volcano's heat—a once-in-a-lifetime experience at a natural wonder.

Hotels cost $118 per night, and round-trip travel averages $340. To escape the muddy, rainy season, come November through March, and it may cost more. Shoulder season visits before November or after March can save money and avoid weather.

Las Vegas (USA)

With the right travel recommendations, flights to Las Vegas are cheap year-round from most regions. CheapAir.com named Sin City one of its best budget-friendly destinations for culture, cuisine, and adventure. Five-star hotels offer rates just over $100, so even low-rollers can afford food and lodging. Budget airlines like Spirit start at $160 round way, plus there's a free shuttle to carry you up and down the Vegas strip.

Arizona's Page

Due to its cheap accommodations and spectacular Arizona road trip landscape, this desert region is the cheapest place to travel. If you want a cheap Western vacation, this northern Arizona town's weekend hotel averages $74 a night. The city is also a great base for exploring Vermilion Cliffs National Park and Rainbow Bridge National Monument, which offer inexpensive outdoor amusement for your vacation.

Flagstaff, a two-hour drive from Page, has more flights and lower prices, averaging $368 round trip. Avoid the hot summer months and crowded national parks. Spring and fall have lower pricing, better weather, and fewer visitors.

Savannah (USA)

Savannah, Georgia, has 22 ancient squares, cobblestone passageways, and Spanish moss-covered oak trees. Pack a picnic and spend an afternoon in Forsyth Park to enjoy the beautiful atmosphere for free. The park's huge, 19th-century cast-iron fountain, built after Paris' Place de la Concorde, is a great place for a free selfie.

The 17-day Savannah Music Festival in spring features jazz, blues, folk, classical, and world roots music for $31. Tybee Island, Savannah's barrier beach, offers magnificent property rentals 15 minutes away. According to the vacation rental platform Home to Go, peak summer home rentals cost $106 per person per night, making them a good deal for groups.

Fun and Free Activities to Enjoy While Traveling on a Budget

Being thrifty doesn't have to mean giving up on fun. Here are some low-cost or no-cost activities you can partake in whenever you need a break from work or school.

Explore Exhibits

There are free days at several tourist attractions, including aquariums, museums, and zoos. On certain days of the year, for instance, Illinois residents can enter the Shedd Aquarium in Chicago for free with proof of residency. The Smithsonian Museums and the National Zoo in Washington, DC, have a free general entry every day of the year. There are also businesses that operate on a "pay what you wish" basis, allowing customers to name their own pricing and others that offer special discounts to members of the military, the elderly, and students.

Your credit or debit card from Bank of America may be your pass. The first weekend of every month, thanks to the bank's "Museum on Us" program, visitors to more than two hundred museums across the country get in free.

Get Lost in a Good Book

Read a new book or reread a classic that you loved. If there are no books on your shelf that interest you, visit the library, make a book trade with a friend, or peruse the used and discounted parts of a bookshop. As an

Amazon Prime member, you have access to thousands of free e-books, periodicals, and comics.

Watch a Film

Check out a DVD from your local library or watch a free film streaming service like Hoopla with your library card. You might also look through the films offered by a reliable free streaming site or the films available through a streaming service you already subscribe to, like Netflix. It is possible to enjoy a trip to the theatre without breaking the bank. If you want to save money on movie tickets, join a loyalty program or go to a matinee.

Have an Indoor Competition

Have some fun with a puzzle, card game, or board game. Check out an app store for low-cost or free video games, or play for fun on a website like Pogo.

Go Outside and Play a Game

In search of some physical activity? Participate in a casual game of basketball in the park, sign up for a local recreational sports league (some are free, while others require a team registration fee), or simply go watch a game.

Donate

There is value in being a helpful neighbor. Free is always a plus. Consider the environment, wildlife, or education as potential topics of interest. Volunteer opportunities can be found by contacting local organizations or using a website like VolunteerMatch.

Go to a Local Farmer's Market

Experience your neighborhood farmers market in all its senses. Locally grown produce has a reputation for being pricey, but it's possible to find it for the same price (or even less!) as grocery store produce. Take a stroll through the market and stop to chat with the merchants and try some of their wares.

Shop at Second-Hand Stores

Look for secondhand and thrift stores for apparel deals. Don't worry; there's no obligation to make a purchase. Just window shopping and trying items on can be entertaining. More frugal buying advice, please! Find out where to look for free apparel.

Take a Stroll

A stroll around the block is now a fun outing, thanks to the proliferation of smartphones, podcasts, and headphones. Taking a walk around the block can help you kill time and get your blood pumping even if you don't have access to high-quality audio.

Go for a Walk

Leave the house and take in the sights and sounds of nature. Find parks and trails in your area by visiting the county or city's website. Then, get a picnic ready, fill up your water bottle, put on your walking shoes, and head outside.

Use a Bicycle

If you have a bike, riding around your neighborhood or along the paths you located on the government website is a quick and enjoyable way to get acquainted with the area. Don't own a bike? You can find gently used models for sale in your area by searching Facebook's Marketplace.

A Night in the Woods

Have a tent and sleeping bag on hand and yearn for additional excitement? Gather up your loved ones and go on a low-cost camping excursion to a predetermined location.

Tune in to Some Tunes

Scan the radio dial or test out a free music service like Spotify or Freegal, which allows you to download tracks with your library card to satisfy your musical needs without breaking the bank. Live performances don't have to break the bank. Find out what's going on and how to save money on concert tickets by checking out event websites and venues.

Want to make some music but don't have any instruments? Not a problem. Get yourself to a music store, pick out a Martin acoustic guitar, and (gently) start strumming away. The staff at a music store is used to the loudness, so feel free to play.

Construct Something

Use your ingenuity to find novel ways to cut costs. You can start a photo album, write a short novel, or cook up something delicious in the kitchen. It's possible that you already own the vast majority of the required resources. If your innovation proves successful, you can use it to launch a side business.

Throw a Potluck Party

Gather your pals and neighbors for a low-key get-together. Create a potluck where each guest contributes a dish, snack, or drink that they are known for. That will lessen the monetary stress placed on the host, who may or may not be you.

Get Some Work Done

Let's face it: we're all putting off something. Schedule some time to organize your home, complete a long-term project, or take care of business. This may involve drafting a will, establishing a budget, organizing a trip, or updating a resume.

Hold a Garage Sale

This alternative is completely free. In all likelihood, your yard sale will turn a profit. Collect all the old stuff you don't want anymore, including clothes and furniture. Then, arrange some tables and welcome the locals to come shop. Eco-friendly junk removal is at your disposal. We can both benefit from that.

Conclusion

As we reach the end of this guide, I hope that you feel inspired, empowered, and eager to embrace the many opportunities and adventures that retirement has to offer. "101exciting Activities to Do in Retirement" was created to provide you with a wealth of ideas, practical tips, and valuable insights to help you make the most of this exciting stage of life. Remember that retirement is not an ending but rather a new beginning – a time for personal growth, exploration, and the pursuit of happiness.

Throughout this book, we've discussed the importance of embracing the freedom of retirement, pursuing lifelong learning, traveling and exploring new places, engaging in hobbies and activities, volunteering and community involvement, prioritizing wellness and self-care, nurturing relationships and social connections, and indulging in creative pursuits and outdoor adventures. We've also provided bonus advice on financial planning, goal-setting, and budget-friendly travel.

As you move forward in your retirement journey, keep these key points in mind:

- Retirement is an amazing stage of life, filled with opportunities for growth, joy, and purpose.
- A wide range of fun and interesting activities awaits you, allowing you to discover new interests and passions in retirement.
- Retirement is the perfect time to explore new opportunities, connect with your community, and find purpose and fulfillment.

The ideas and suggestions presented in this book are just a starting point. Your retirement experience is unique, and the possibilities are truly endless. Stay curious, be open to new experiences, and never stop learning. As you continue to grow and explore, you will undoubtedly find even more ways to enjoy your retirement and make the most of every moment.

In closing, I want to thank you for allowing me to be a part of your retirement journey. I'm honored to have been able to share my experiences, insights, and passion with you. As you embark on this new chapter of life, remember that the adventure has just begun. Embrace the opportunities, cherish the memories, and above all, enjoy the ride.

Here's to a fulfilling, fun, and unforgettable retirement!

Made in the USA
Monee, IL
15 June 2023

35926281R00066